ME ME ME

CHARLOTTE CROSBY

ME ME ME

CHARLOTTE CROSBY

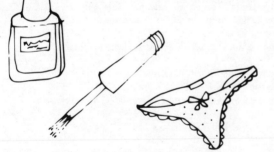

headline

First published in 2015
by HEADLINE PUBLISHING GROUP

6

Cataloguing in Publication Data is available from the British Library

Hardback ISBN 978 1 4722 2966 3
Trade Paperback ISBN 978 1 4722 3063 8
Typeset in Berling by Palimpsest Book Production Ltd, Falkirk, Stirlingshire

Printed and bound in Great Britain by Clays Ltd, St Ives plc

Headline's policy is to use papers that are natural, renewable and
recyclable products and made from wood grown in sustainable forests.
The logging and manufacturing processes are expected to conform to
the environmental regulations of the country of origin.

HEADLINE PUBLISHING GROUP
An Hachette UK Company
Carmelite House
50 Victoria Embankment
London EC4 0DZ

www.headline.co.uk
www.hachette.co.uk

To my Mam, Dad, Nathaniel and all my family and friends, with love and thanks for being the best support network a girl could wish for!

Contents

Introduction

THIS iS ME (ME, ME)

Oh, hello there! Hope you're having a good day. So here I am, writing my own book! Well, I never thought *that* would happen.

If only my teacher Mrs Wallace could see me now – all those times I was told off in maths for singing stupid songs! Now look at me, I have an actual book that I can do what I want with. I might even make up a song right now, you know, just to kick things off a bit. . .

A Song for my Reader
(To be rapped, in a gangsta way)

As you turn each page of this book,
You'll probably think 'WHAT THE FUCK?'
But fear not! Don't be alarmed!
At the end of this book you might be quite charmed,
But until then sit back, HOLD TIGHT!
I'm about to talk a load of shite!

Anyway, welcome, dear reader . . . to my life! Hopefully you already know a bit about me – the name's Charlotte Letitia Crosby. I'm twenty-five years old (well, at the time of writing this anyway; you might be reading this book in years to come – as a piece of history – and I could be sixty-five by now). I'm in a programme on MTV called *Geordie Shore* where it's my job to get proper mortal and do crazy things. I was the winner of *Celebrity Big Brother* in 2013 (even though I wet the bed on telly), I've got a fitness DVD called *Charlotte Crosby's 3-Minute Belly Blitz* and my bum has been projected onto the Houses of Parliament (I tell people I did a moony right into David Cameron's office). I like to think I'm a pretty good person – I haven't murdered anyone or anything. And I love nothing more in the world than seeing people laugh, preferably at something I've done to entertain them.

I have quite a lot of bad habits. So I might as well get them out of the way now:

1. Compulsive nose picking
2. Chewing with my mouth open
3. Farting constantly
4. Washing my bits with baby wipes because I can't be bothered to shower
5. Scratching my bum hole
6. Sniffing pages of books
7. Twitching my nose a lot
8. Eating loudly like a wild boar
9. Drinking gravy
10. Snoring
11. Pissing the bed

I have to confess I've never read anyone else's autobiography the whole way through because (*whisper it*) I'm never all that interested in what they have to say. I always think to myself, 'Why on earth would I want to read a book about the likes of Spencer Matthews? What the hell has happened in their life that's so entertaining that I'm going to *really* want to know about?'

So now you must be thinking, 'So why the hell is Charlotte Crosby writing one?!'

Well, I'll tell you why. Because this one's going to be different. I'm going to skim past all the boring bits (like the stuff about how me mam and dad first met and what me nana used to make me for tea) and just tell you the things *I'd* want to read about if I was *you*. Like the first

time I got pubes, how many times I've been arrested and how many drinks it takes me to get proper mortal.

So by way of introduction I thought I'd tell you about some of the key people in my life and what they would say if I asked them to describe me. On the subject of people in my life, there are a few names in this book that have been changed. Newcastle is a very small place and I don't want any ex-boyfriends getting mad at what I've had to say about them and deciding to throw eggs at my house!

First, there's **me mam and dad: Letitia and Gary Crosby.** I wouldn't be able to survive without Letitia – she washes all my clothes, buys my food, irons for me, tidies my room, washes and dries my hair (yes, even now aged twenty-five), books me in for a smear test and a dentist appointment whenever I need one and is always on hand for advice.

Me dad, Gary, helps with the things Letitia might freak out about (like carrying me down off the roof when I'm up there because I'm too mortal) – he's the sensible one. Dad helps me with all the more intelligent sides to life (because if I'm honest me mam's a bit thick). Dad knows what to do with money, tax and all the stuff that I wouldn't have a clue about.

Without me mam and dad I'd be well and truly fucked.

And if they were to describe me? Dad would say, 'Charlotte's a bit lapsidaisy, she's very dozy and stupid and you can't really trust her with anything.' While Mam would say, 'She's lovely and kind-hearted and beautiful.' Mam is a big softie and my biggest fan. I can do *anything* and she'll stick up for me.

Then there's **my little brother Nathaniel**. There are fifteen years between us but he's the most fun person in the world. When I'm at home in Sunderland (where I still live if I'm not working in London), I'd be bored shitless without him. We run around and pretend we're in armies and shoot each other and wrestle on the bed. If he were to try to describe me he'd say I'm the best sister in the world ☺.

Nana Jean, Granddad Tommy and Nana Doreen: Jean and Tommy are me mam's parents and Nana Doreen is Dad's mam. Both nanas are really small and cute (why is it that old people look so cute? I think they must shrink because they probably weren't cute when they were younger) and Jean would say, 'Ooh, the Charlotte on TV isn't the one I know, she was always such a nice child.' While Doreen would just love everything I did because she worships the ground I walk on. Granddad Tommy (who wears tracksuits and sovereign rings and always makes me laugh) would just disagree with whatever me Nana Jean said because they used to be married and still argue about *everything* to this day.

Next it's **my best friends**. I've got a small group of best friends who I've known since junior school – **Anna, Beka, Christina, Laura, Lauren, Natalie, Katie and Melissa**. We've been mates since I was four years old. I've got a lot of good friends but I spend the most time with Melissa. She's a makeup artist, which means she can travel around with me on jobs giving me false eyelashes and a tan. She's a big part of my life. Melissa would say, 'Charlotte's an idiot, unorganised, late, always a mess, never makes an effort but is crazy and very funny.'

Then it's **Mitch**: he's **my boyfriend**. We've been together on and off for two and a half years and I think I'll be with Mitch for the rest of my life. I definitely want him to be the father of my children and we're talking about getting a house together in London soon so he *has* to be a key part of my life. If I was to ask him to describe me he'd probably say, 'She has a cute forehead and I love her but she can be a bit irritating.'

(If I was to ask any of my *ex*-boyfriends to describe me they'd say: 'A psychopath, very funny, really bad news.')

To give you a bit more of an insight into Charlotte Crosby world, here's some stuff I've done that maybe I shouldn't:

- Running away from home and sleeping in my car for two weeks
- Having sex on TV
- Trying to jump off the roof at me mam and dad's house
- Turning up to work in my pyjamas
- Trying cigarettes for the first time
- Skiving off school *a lot*
- Drinking at the age of seventeen on the streets and then having to go to hospital to get my stomach pumped
- Getting locked up numerous times
- Rolling in my own poo

Here are some things that make me laugh:

- All of the above and . . .
- People falling over – there have been so many good falls in *Geordie Shore*. One of the best was when Holly was running round the corner on a boat we were staying on in Amsterdam and as she slid you could hear the connection on the floor afterwards – it was so loud! And there was one night when Marnie fell all the way down the stairs in the *Geordie Shore* house in series ten and it was hilarious!

Here are some things guaranteed to make me cry:

- Break-ups
- Boys who cheat on their girlfriends
- Old people – I don't like seeing them by themselves, it makes me really sad
- Bullying – I hate people being bullied. It makes me so mad if I see anyone getting picked on. I want to run over and sort it out

And some things I've been taught not to do:

- Swear – Dad doesn't like it and we're never allowed to swear at home
- Talk to strangers – I've always been taught never to speak to people I don't know. Only problem is, now I have to be out in the world on my own (and I'm always pissed) it's hard not to break that rule. I always get asked for photos with people I don't know so I don't have any choice
- Be rude – my parents have always told me the import-ance of saying 'please' and 'thank you' and I'm also quite good at gauging what to say to people so I don't hurt anyone's feelings. I'm a very honest person but sometimes honesty is not the best policy (not if it means offending someone and knocking their confidence).

1

THE SAVIOUR IS BORN

There was a girl named Charlotte
We found her on the street.
We put her into Geordie Shore
And she found it a real treat.

Drinking, shaggin', partying
Was all she had to do
And then she went and impressed us
All with her massive love of poo!

She shit herself on national TV
And not just the once,
But as we went and showed it all
She thinks we're massive c**ts.

But the nation saw and loved it
And called it 'TV gold',
And now you could be more famous
If you just did what you were told.

This was a poem written about me by a guy called Dan McGowan, the assistant producer on *Geordie Shore*. He wrote it in my memory book. I keep everything important and funny in my memory book just so I don't forget things that have happened to me (I've also got a sanitary pad in there to mark my first period of 2010 and all the pubes of my fellow housemates from *Celebrity Big Brother 2013*). But I'm jumping ahead a bit. First I need to get you interested in this thing called 'my life'. . .

I've been told that every good book needs a 'hook' – a 'catchy intro'. Something that's going to get you so engrossed you don't want to put it down. It's not just books either – when you watch a TV programme or a film, if it's got a boring beginning then you'll switch over or leave the cinema (or snog the boy next to you for the whole film instead, which wouldn't be such a bad thing). So I've decided to treat the story of my life like it's a piece of art (obviously

2

me mam would argue that I am 'art' because she thinks everything I do is perfect).

With that in mind, I've worked out a few different treatments of how the story of Charlotte Crosby began. . .

1.   THE FILM TRAILER

The scene opens in the delivery room. There's a misty colour all over the screen like they have in romantic movies. There's always romance and intrigue in a film, but if this film trailer is about the beginning of my life it obviously can't be me having the romance because I'm only a small baby. And I don't even have one pube yet. So the romance in this trailer takes place between the midwife and the doctor.

At the side of the frame is a glamorous-looking midwife. She's licking her lips and looking all seductively at the camera. Behind her is a doctor writing notes and looking up at her, hoping she will notice his stare burning into the back of her midwife's outfit. In the middle of the room on an operating table is me mam, legs spread. And baby Charlotte is about to burst out into the world. . .

Actually this one isn't going to work. Because if the midwife and the doctor are about to have it away with each other then what's happening to poor me? I might be forgotten about in all this steamy passion. And I'm the most important one in this story!

Let's try again. . .

2.   THE BIBLE

In the beginning, way before iPhones, God blessed a womb – and not just any womb. The womb of Letitia Crosby, my mother. Little did Letitia know she was about to give birth to 'the Saviour'. She was with her husband Gary, who was an operations manager (not quite a carpenter but never mind). And they travelled to Sunderland, a city in Bethlehem on a donkey – just like the one in Shrek, he talked too much – and lo and behold, Letitia popped out: a baby in a stable in a manger. Which was a bit like a Pret a Manger but it was full of hay instead of sandwiches. The child was called Charlotte, which in the Urban Dictionary means: 'The girl who is known for being beautiful inside and out' (it also says 'usually on the shy side; can come across as boring' but they got that bit wrong). They wrapped her in swaddling clothes (which are like onesies but not quite as cool) and three wise men came to bring her gifts. They were called Ant, Dec and David Walliams. A star shone above them and everyone knew she was special because her skin was shining in the light – a brilliant shade of mahogany.

Actually, this isn't going to work either. I'm meant to be the Saviour, someone who gives her life to the whole world, yet I'm being born in a stable with a donkey? I expect more VIP treatment than that! So let's try something else, something made for TV . . .

3. THE ADVERT

The woman is hot, she's sweating. The camera pans to her vagina, everyone's stressed and panicking around her and all of a sudden, music blares and out emerges . . . Charlotte Crosby. I'm like super baby (think Stewie from Family Guy*). I'm wearing really cool high heels. Nothing fazes me. People around are still flapping at what's happened. But without even looking round behind me, I hand me mam a tissue to wipe her brow. Then a hand comes into shot to spray my hair, someone puts some lipstick on me . . . I walk closer to the camera and then I wink, flick my hair and say, 'Because I'm worth it.'*

Now that's better! I think people would buy into that, wouldn't they?

OK, now I've reeled you in. Let's get started. . .

Let's begin with Letitia Crosby, me mam. She's forty-seven but looks thirty-five. She's got long dark hair and tiny squinty eyes that almost disappear into her head and she's got so many freckles all over her body she's like a join-the-dots book. Letitia is a brilliant mum. Me dad Gary is as big as a tree and reminds me of the tall skinny one in *The Simpsons* . . . what's his name again? Montgomery Burns – that's it! Me dad is just like him, but not quite as thin. He loves cycling and football and has tried to do my fitness DVD a few times but he's too long and gangly to do my girlie moves.

These days I don't get to be in Sunderland as much as I'd like, but when I am home Letitia does everything for me and treats me like a princess. She says I have a 'rider' – like one of those demanding celebrities when they go to different hotels – because I like my bedroom to have the air of a boutique hotel with crisp white sheets and fresh tulips in a vase on my bedside table. Problem is I'm so messy that I can destroy three rooms within five minutes (and I mean *blitz* them). Dad always looks at the place when I've walked in and says it's like we've been burgled eight times over. When I'm in the bath she will sit on the toilet so she can talk to me, then she washes, dries and styles my hair for me (I manage to convince her that she's better at doing it than I am), and then does my fake tan. It's like having my own personal assistant and I don't know what I'd do without her. She loves it, though. Mam says she's dreading the day that I leave for good and buy my own house in London. She says she won't be able to stop crying.

No Knickers

Me mam hasn't always been that attentive, though. When I was a little kid she used to forget to put knickers on me. Here's how a typical day would go when I was aged four: we'd wake up late which means Mam would be rushing to get me ready for school. When we got there she'd wave me goodbye, then I'd trot into the classroom and before long I'd be dancing on the tables (I got some practice in early on!). It didn't take long before people started noticing that something was missing. So me mam got called into the school and was told by the teachers that she really needed to start putting underwear on her daughter. But I didn't like it. I'd been so free before! Knickers were *very* restricting. I think that explains a lot about how I ended up the way I am today.

The Toilet

As well as not being all that keen on knickers, I don't like having a poo on my own either. Me dad always tries closing the door when I'm on the toilet or Mam starts shouting, 'Shut the door, Charlotte!' But I tell them I can't because I get claustrophobic. Well actually, I don't, it's a lie, I just say that so I can keep the door open so I know what's going on. I like to be able to join in the conversation at all times.

Bad Teeth

As a child I wasn't blessed with a good set of teeth. They were big. And by big I mean BIG. Think of a rabbit and then put those rabbit teeth on a young girl. People in school called me Gretchen, which was the name of a cartoon character with big goofy teeth and glasses. It never fazed me, though, I knew they were a bit oversized but I wasn't that bothered by it. I don't remember ever looking in the mirror and worrying about my appearance. That wasn't me. Me mam was obviously worried, though – which is why she decided I had to have a brace when I was twelve. This meant I was a bit of a late developer because while everyone else was kissing boys I had train-tracks in my mouth. And no boy wanted to kiss *them* in case they got their face stuck in there for ever. There was one nasty boy who used to bully me a bit and call me goofy. He was called Tommy Adams and he's probably in prison now – '*Hi Tommy, if you're reading this, hope your cell's nice and has a microwave.*' Sometimes he would run after me on the way home from school. But I was never scared. I think my teeth had superpowers.

Pets

I've always loved animals; I think I have a good connection with them and can communicate with them in their language (the two fish I bought in *Geordie Shore* called Scramble and Egg were like my best mates). We had loads of different pets when I was younger – there was a hamster and a guinea pig called Raz. Once I went into the sitting room to see my dad and said, 'Do you like my hat?' and I had my guinea pig on my head. One day I came home with two rabbits I'd got in the pet shop – I thought they were a couple but it turned out they were two boys who kept trying to hump each other. I think me mam must've put something in their food because they got massive and used to break out of the hutch and go round the estate eating out of people's gardens. In the end Mam got fed up of looking out of the window and seeing them humping each other all over the back garden, so she gave them away. They were at it so much they literally hopped about with sperm all over their faces. People were beginning to talk.

Friends

I was an only child until my brother Nathaniel was born when I was fifteen. I was very sociable and had loads of mates. The good thing was, when I got bored of them I had another friend who wasn't actually real – she was a girl called Polly who would come out of my hand every time I went to the toilet at school. She was tiny. I remember being on the loo and speaking to Polly on the palm of my hand. She was like a toy Polly Pocket but she was alive. I don't really know why this Polly only came out when I was on the loo. Maybe she knew I didn't like being there on my own, or she wanted to check I was having a poo. Anyway, for the record, Polly had a pink top and a navy blue skirt.

As for my actual human friends – they're people I'm still friends with to this day. Laura was a black belt in karate who we called 'the German girl' (she wasn't even German, I just think she'd been there for a few days once).

Christina was my 'hard friend'; she was more mature for her age and wore makeup and jewellery all the time. She was also the one who smoked and was the first of us to have a boyfriend.

Lauren was my sidekick. We both had bad teeth – she had one long tooth and I had braces – and she never kissed any boys for ages because she was too scared.

Anna didn't go to our school; she was Christina's cousin and was a bit younger than us. She always used to try and come out with us and was a bit of a pest until we got older!

Beka is an enigma. She actually didn't go to any of my schools so it's a mystery as to how I became friends with her. She's one of my best friends but still, to this day, I honestly don't know how we met!

Melissa was always messing about with me in class and we'd often get separated because of it. We spent most of our time in detention.

Katie was one of my best mates at school; we were in all the same classes and everyone fancied her. I was always the ugly funny friend and we spent most of our time laughing.

And then there was Natalie, who looked like she had too many teeth for her face. Natalie was so outgoing and when I met her I was really shy. On the first day at school she was strutting around talking to everyone and suddenly she wiggled her forefinger in my face and said to me, 'Can you do this with your finger?' I shrugged and said, 'Yeah,' and she smiled: 'Good, we've got something in common then.' Natalie was the funny one and once I came out of my shell I used to compete with her about who could be the most fun. My friends still try and wind me up about it now and are always saying things like, 'Natalie's being hilarious today.' She is bloody funny, though. She can do loads of accents and they have me in stitches.

Our gang in school was called the DCR: the Dancing Crew Rejects. This was because the popular gang in school – the really pretty ones – would dance *all* the time and we'd stand next to them doing stupid moves.

No Boys Allowed

I went to an all-girls' school called St Anthony's in Sunderland and it was very religious. I loved being at all-girls' school because you never had to dress up to impress boys. Holly from *Geordie Shore* told me that she went to a mixed school. She said, 'Every day I'd wear a thong and I'd pull it right up behind my skirt so all the boys could see in the row behind.' Eh? A thong! I was still wearing a vest and granny knickers set from Asda until I was about fifteen! All I cared about was having a laugh with my mates and messing about in class.

My favourite teacher was Mrs Wallace, who taught maths. She was really skinny and had a thick head of hair in a bob, like Lego hair. And she had a very shrill voice that could grate cheese. I always played up in her class but I know that secretly she loved me. I used to make up random songs and perform them to my mates and I'd do this thing where I'd flick chewing gum into the sky and it would land on the tables. I'd always get into trouble but I think she only gave me detention so she could spend more time with me.

Sister Francis taught RE and was the sweetest little nun in the world. She was always there to offer advice. The problem is everyone took the piss out of her because she was too nice.

The head teacher was called Sister Mildred and everyone was scared of her. Then there was Bulldog, the dinner lady. We called her that because she genuinely did look like one and she used to stand guard at the gates just like a dog. But we'd always jump over the walls and go out for dinner in break times. We'd go into town, steal sandwiches from Greggs and put them in the lining of our blazers. Then we'd walk back into school with a load of crumbs in our coats. We loved the freedom of going out for dinner instead of having to go to the canteen. The FREEDOM OF GREGGS! Bulldog caught us a couple of times but we used to outrun her.

Clothes

I used to dress like a right charva (that's what we call chavs in Newcastle). The uniform would go like this: hair scraped back with two little strands pulled out, tracksuit bottoms, Rockport trainers and Fred Perry striped jumpers. Basically everyone modelled themselves on Vicky Pollard from *Little Britain*.

Me mam used to try her hardest to make me look like a proper girl – she'd dress me in denim jackets and little leather pleated skirts and I'd moan and say, 'I can't go out like this!' So I'd get changed when she wasn't looking. I was never very good at doing my makeup though. I wore this white eye shadow that made me look like I had Tipp-Ex on my eyes.

Skiving School

My mate Lauren's mam worked in the school canteen. Her job meant she was at home most of the day so when we wanted to skive off school (which I'm sorry to say we did quite often), we had to hide in the cupboard until she left the house. Lauren lived really close to the school which meant I could pretend to me mam that I was walking to class when really I was walking to a secret hiding place. Me and Lauren spent days in that cupboard and it became really quite homely – it was long and ran under the stairs and we put loads of blankets in there. We used to lie down and use our phones, write letters and draw stuff. To this day, if you look in Lauren's mam's cupboard you'll see things like 'Charlotte loves Titch' scrawled all over the walls.

There was no way Lauren's mam would ever guess we'd be in there either. The cupboard entrance was usually blocked with a wardrobe so we'd have to push the wardrobe out of the way to get in and then slide our bodies inside. The only times we were able to roam the house was when Lauren's mam was at work between 12 and 2 p.m. One day her mam came back earlier than expected because she wasn't feeling very well. There was a mad panic and Lauren managed to quickly squeeze herself back inside the cupboard. But we hadn't moved the wardrobe out that far so when I tried to slide my body back in, only half of it would fit and the door closed on my neck leaving my head dangling out! We were trying our hardest to be quiet so we wouldn't get caught but we were laughing so much (you know that silent laughter that never ends up being very silent?) that I started to wee myself. It was the first of many times I was to lose control of my bladder: I was weeing all down my legs and it was dribbling all over the floorboards towards where Lauren was crouching. All the time we were trying not to make a sound in case her mam went upstairs and saw my head hanging out of her cupboard door. Luckily she'd gone to have a sleep on the settee so in the end we managed to sneak out of the house altogether. I don't think Lauren's mam ever found out we used to be secret cupboard dwellers . . . well, not until she read this book.

CHARLOTTE'S WORDS OF WISDOM ON: RELIGION

I went to an all-girls' Catholic school, so I know the whole religious thing is pretty simple . . .

Some girl called Mary got pregnant and she hadn't even had sex yet (pretty unlucky), but her kid happened to be the Son of God, so she was probably buzzing. Just like a WAG, this meant she was set up for life. Her son Jesus is then born and turns out he can do all these magical things like feed the 500 with one loaf of bread (he's kind of like Harry Potter). All he wants to do is teach people the honest and good way of life, but just like these days not everyone wants to listen. To be honest, Jesus was absolutely mint. I bet he was a dead canny lad. Such a shame no one believed he was the Son of God! I wish I was alive back then because I would have believed him and I would have loved to have been his girlfriend.

2

BECOMING A WOMAN: MY FIRST PUBE

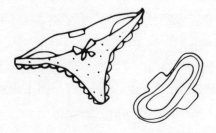

I was about fourteen or fifteen when I started to have sexual feelings.

Me mam and dad used to watch the comedian character Ali G on telly; they thought he was hilarious and would sit there laughing their heads off. Someone bought them an Ali G book for Christmas . . . and in the back there were diagrams of sex positions and sketches of a real-life penis! It was hidden in the cupboard but I used to get it out when no one was watching. I'd look at the pictures and think 'Whoa!'. I knew it was rude because it had been hidden (which obviously made me go and look at it *all* the time) and when I read it I got weird feelings down *there*, but I didn't tell anyone.

There was also a show on telly called *Nip/Tuck* about these men who were plastic surgeons and I liked it because they sometimes had sex in the show. I used to sneak it on my TV late at night when Mam and Dad thought I was asleep and I'd put the volume on really low so no one could hear. I used to feel really weird when I watched it and got a nice tingly feeling. That's when I realised there was something out there that I needed to discover.

Maybe I experienced those feelings a bit earlier, too, as sometimes when I'd be in school, I'd brush my fairy (the name I gave my vagina) past the corners of the tables because I liked the sensation it gave me. I'd stand there sharpening my pencil and I'd be rubbing up and down on the corner of the table! I was quite secretive about it so I don't think the teacher ever noticed. It used to feel NICE! But I was too young to realise what I was doing back then.

What I didn't ever need to discover though, was me mam and dad having sex. I remember hearing them at it and I wanted to cry. I heard noises and banging coming from their room and I used to put my head under my pillow. I knew there was something weird going on and I didn't like it.

Mam worked in a sandwich shop called the Lunchbox and for years I'd walk there after school. Me and Lauren used to wind her up all the time and one day she tried to get her own back: 'Charlotte, you spend so much time with Lauren lately people might think you're a lesbian.'

'Well, I know you're not a lesbian because I heard you having sex and it made me want to cry under my pillow!' I retorted.

'Oh my God, Charlotte!' Mam was gutted.

'Yeah, you should be upset, Mam. It was awful for me. I'll never get those memories out of my head!'

Because I went to an all-girls' school, all everyone talked about was what it would be like having sex with a boy and anyone who'd actually *done* it was seen as really cool. I think it was because we rarely saw boys, which meant the opportunity for fornication (as the nuns called it) didn't present itself very often. So if you'd actually had sex with a boy everyone looked up to you (which is pretty warped now I come to think of it).

I wasn't anywhere near doing *that* yet, though. Me and Natalie spent most of our time at school in a pretend band called 'The Naked Marchers' – although we were never actually naked.

One of our songs went like this:

Sexual positions are easy as additions
Do do do do do do do do
Up and down and all around
Do do do do do do do do
Left to right, easy as shite
Do do do do do do do do

Under the sheet, to the beat
Do do do do do do do do
Sexual positions are easy as additions

It was a short song, but very effective.

Everyone loved our songs; we constantly practised them in the playground. Natalie's brother was in a proper band and he played the guitar in the background of one of the songs and it sounded amazing. I'd still love to be in a band – but not a real one, a parody one a bit like *Flight of the Conchords*.

There was an underage midweek disco called Lush (Mam called them 'nappy nights') in Sunderland and that's where we got to mingle with actual boys. It was at Lush that I had my first kiss. And it was a disaster.

All the pretty girls would spend the night having kissing competitions to see who could snog the most boys in one night. But me and my mate Lauren both had braces – and of course no one wanted to kiss a brace face. We were too scared to do anything anyway; we had massive cock fright and preferred just having a laugh with our mates and watching from the sidelines. But the pressure started piling on; the other girls were on their eighth and ninth boys in a row and were looking at us saying, 'Come on! Your turn now!'

My first kiss was a *bad* experience. The boy in question was called Liam and was small and ugly but I just thought, 'I need to get it out of the way – he'll have to do.' The problem was, at nappy nights there was no such thing as a secret smooch – people thought everything was their business and if someone was doing any kissing then everyone else would stand around and watch. So there I was, trying to do the deed with Liam and before I knew it I had a swarm of people around me waiting to watch my move. It was my first kiss, I had an audience and I didn't even know what I was doing!

So I took the plunge but as I lent in to kiss him, Liam started bending backwards. It was like I was the man and he was the woman – I was cradling him in my arms like a baby! Then it happened: dead fast, like a washing machine. The next day the rumours went round school – 'Charlotte nearly broke a boy's back last night kissing him.' After that I vowed I'd get some practice in before I did anything again in public.

Anna Taylor, one of the hard girls at school who had the benefit of also being quite pretty, was one of the first people I knew to have a proper boyfriend and she would always boast about getting the morning-after pill. I didn't have a clue what that was. I thought it was some kind of Ecstasy and really dangerous. I'd sit there and think, 'If my mam knew I was going to have the morning-after pill she'd kill me. I'd probably get locked up!'

People started smoking cigarettes, too. My friend Christina smoked first because that's what all the cool girls did in school. One day I said, 'Can I have a try?' and it was absolutely awful. I sucked it right back and I couldn't stop

21

coughing and went all dizzy and light-headed. Then another rumour went round school: 'Charlotte fainted off a cigarette.'

I honestly don't see what the big deal is with smoking. It's horrible. I tried it again when I was drunk filming *Geordie Shore* once and it was disgusting. It gives you the most horrible taste in the back of your throat and the next morning when you wake up, your mouth still has that awfulness and it makes you feel sick.

Obviously all this messing about was just our way of trying to prove we were grown up. But the biggest sign of *that* was getting your first period. I got mine on Pancake Day and I was twelve. I remember sitting in Maths and I had really bad stomach pains. I didn't know what it could be and never for a minute thought it could be my period. When I got home, Mam was making pancakes and all of a sudden I felt a dampness in my knickers and thought I was wetting myself (which as I've grown up has become quite a common occurrence). I knew I needed to go to the toilet. I got into the loo, pulled down my pants and was faced with a pool of red blood. *Oh.* I knew it was a big thing because Letitia had always gone on about how getting your period means you're becoming a woman. But all I could think was, 'I've got to go and tell Mam – and it will ruin the whole pancake atmosphere!'

You see, Mam goes all emotional and weird about stuff like that. So I knew it would upset the balance of what should have been a nice evening eating pancakes. And I *loved* pancakes. Why did it need to happen on Pancake Day of all days?!

Nervously I made my way out to the kitchen. Mam was at the cooker with her back to me; she was poised, about to flip a pancake. I stood there, knickers round my ankles, took a deep breath and said, 'Mam . . . look!'

The flip didn't happen.

The pancake was ruined.

It looked like scrambled egg in a pan.

Mam started crying, she lost concentration and there and then we had to have the tampon talk. I was marched off to the bathroom and she stood behind the door awkwardly trying to instruct me how to put one in. She was whispering through the bathroom door . . .

'Have you got the tip in?'

'Yes! Leave me alone!'

'Is it in?'

'Stop it, Mam! I'll tell you when it's in!'

'Do you want me to come and help you?'

'No! What are you? Some kind of lesbian?!"

After what seemed like about an hour I finally got it up there then turned to Mam and said, 'I don't like this, it hurts.' So she bought me some sanitary pads instead, which just made me look like I was wearing a nappy.

It wasn't just all about periods. There were pubes too. For some reason, as soon as the little wiry things started to grow, Lauren and me would sit against the radiator and pluck them all out. Every Saturday we'd get a pair of tweezers, go up to Lauren's spare room and pluck away. It would take us ages and we'd be there for hours.

'Are you nearly done?'

'No I've still got *loads*!'

The minute they grew back we'd say to each other, 'I need to pluck me pubes.'

'Yeah, me too.'

'Shall we do it this weekend?'

'Yeah.'

And that was the extent of our weekend: pube plucking.

CHARLOTTE'S WORDS OF WISDOM ON: FRIENDS

The good thing about friends is that YOU can pick THEM (unlike your family who you are stuck with!). But what you have to understand is that not every human being is perfect. Friends should be your friends because you love them no matter what their good and bad points are. Everyone has bad points but if you fell out with them each time they did something that annoyed you then you would have no friends at all.

My best friends:

Anna (the worrier) – Anna worries *all the time* about the stupidest things; she's either constantly stressed or constantly worried. When we all have a night out and she gets too drunk and does something embarrassing she will worry about it all the next day. It's so annoying – but because she's my friend I just have to love her and accept her for her good and her bad sides and reassure her that it's fine that the woman who put her in the ambulance for being too drunk and had to change her tampon for her *while she was passed out* is just a random woman and she will never have to see her again.

Laura (the angry one) – Laura went through a very moody stage in her teenage years and would get very angry about everything and anything, but because I love her for who she is we just had to be the ones to calm her down and try and persuade her that it was a great idea to come out with us and to try and *not* smash her bedroom up just because she's lost her other eyelash in the carpet. Come to think of it, after reading this book she may want to set it on fire.

Mel (the clumsy one) – Mel breaks everything and has a tendency to either trample on me or swing me around when she's drunk! And although at times I've woken up with a huge egg on my head from her drunkenly falling into me and me smacking my head on the wall, I just have to remember she's my friend and I love her for her good and bad qualities and this gigantic bump on my forehead will make for a great story to passers by.

Christina (the womanly one) – Since we were about twelve, Christina was always the womanly one. She had huge boobs and lovely tanned skin and all the boys ALWAYS fancied her! She was perfect in every way. She was really popular as well and the 'hard girls' kind of accepted her into their group too. It's tough to find bad points about Christina. . .

Natalie (the funny one) – Natalie is so funny, soooo funny, that all of the other girls laugh at her and always say that she is the funniest out of our group of friends and even though it fills me with rage and makes me want to tape her mouth up so she can never be funny again (because I want to be the funniest), I have to love her because she is my friend. I laugh every time she tells her jokes when really a pit of hell burns in my belly every time. LOL.

Lauren (the online shopper) – Lauren always spends all of her money on clothes and then has no money to do fun things. But I suppose at least it means we get to borrow nice things when the rest of us go out without her!

Beka (the disappearing act) – Beka's the friend who always has a boyfriend and when she does she never comes out much, but because I love her, I just have to accept her for her good and bad points and remember that she's there when it matters.

Geordie Shore **pals:**
Holly (the diva) – Holly is a massive DIVA and she will admit that herself. When we're filming *Geordie Shore* she will sometimes just refuse to do things and has to have almost everything her way! But I have to accept her for her good and bad points and realise maybe it's a blessing that Holly kicks off about certain things because then it gets me out of them as well (because me and Holly do everything together!).

Sophie (the moaner) – Sophie is the world's worst moaner! She will moan about everything and anything, she's like an old woman. She's a little bit of a liar as well . . . I remember when we were in Australia and she lied on her medical form saying she had asthma just so she could use it as an excuse to get out of doing shit things she didn't want to do. We were in the villa, just me, her and her boyfriend Joel and the producers came in and said, 'Great news, guys! Today you are going to swim with sharks!' We were all buzzing – 'Wooooooooo!' – until they turned around and said, 'Oh Sophie, you can't go, you have asthma.' She was furious and kicked off and tried to tell them she was lying but they didn't believe her. Anyway, to cut a long story short, she got in a huge mood with Joel for experiencing swimming with sharks with me and *not her*. BUT I have to remember she's my friend and I love her for everything and she is practically my sister.

The conclusion to all this is that every friend has good and bad points, so you have to just accept them with all their faults otherwise you won't have any friends at all and then you will just be Billy No Mates. And nobody wants to be Billy.

3

MORTAL MEMORIES

As we got older, 'nappy nights' became less about innocent kissing and more about getting pissed without our
parents knowing. Or so we thought. One of the girls had
an older brother who would go to the shop and get us vodka
or cider and we'd drink it in the back lane before we went
inside. We always thought he was really mysterious. He wore
hoodies and never really spoke much. We'd sometimes creep
into his room when he wasn't in and he'd have all these
Nuts magazines with pictures of women's boobs in them.

I still remember the first time I ever got pissed – it was

such a weird feeling – all dizzy and spinny. Isn't it funny how you don't ever feel like that again?

Cider was our favourite drink. We'd have a litre before we went into nappy nights and we'd be proper mortal. One evening me mam came and picked us up and on the way home she kept demanding to know if I'd been drinking (it was pretty obvious – I was slurring all over the place) and because I denied it she drove me to the police station! She said she could smell it on my breath. 'Tell me now what you've been drinking otherwise I'm going to tell the police and you'll be locked up.' So I had to come clean.

Apart from that, during the ages of fifteen and sixteen, me mam and dad were convinced I was being a good girl and behaving myself while the rest of my mates were off getting pissed and into trouble. I'd come home from school and tell them both stories of people like Christina and Lauren getting proper mortal and having to be carried home just so I could suss out their reaction. I wanted to test how they responded because the truth was that I was doing it too (and I was probably the worst one!). Whenever I said anything about what my mates had been up to they'd be really disappointed. They'd sit on the settee, look at each other and say, 'At least Charlotte's not like that.' So I knew I couldn't admit what I was *really* getting up to.

Instead they had to find out with a phone call . . . from Sunderland Hospital.

I don't actually remember much of it myself. All I can visualise is being in a dressing gown trying to run away down

30

a corridor and being chased by a nurse! Me mam and dad have a slightly clearer recollection of events however . . .

Dad was on a nightshift at work – an electronics plant that made computer chips – when he got the phone call from me mam.

'Charlotte's in hospital,' Letitia shrieked down the phone.

'Oh no, what's wrong?' Gary was worried.

'She's pissed!'

I was fifteen.

Dad was so upset he had to go and ask his boss if he could go home. The news that his beautiful daughter Charlotte, the one he had been convinced was so innocent and pure, was now so drunk she'd had to be taken to hospital, had hit him hard. He was so shocked he didn't know how to cope with it.

That evening, when he thought I was tucked up watching telly at Lauren's house, I had in fact been hanging around a place called South Hilton in a field near a graveyard with a load of friends drinking cheap cider and running around like a lunatic. I was absolutely mortal. So mortal that when the time came for everyone else to go home, I'd passed out and no one could get me up. They tried to drag me – *in my white jeans!* – across the grass without much luck. In the end one of them called for an ambulance and I had to get my stomach pumped.

Me mam and Nana Jean came to pick me up. Nana Jean was there because Mam was eight months' pregnant with my brother Nathaniel at the time and she was so massive.

(Honestly, you want to have seen me mam's belly! It was sooo big it was like she had a full UFO spaceship inside her. She had green and blue veins all over her stomach.) She could hardly do anything, let alone come and rescue her drunken fifteen-year-old daughter.

I think I was still pissed when they got there, because I can't remember much apart from mumbling, 'I'm sorry!' as my poor pregnant mam picked up my grass-stained jeans from the chair and desperately tried to lift me up and get me into the car.

I'd like to say I learnt to hold my liquor after that. But you'd know that would be a big fat lie. Within weeks I was at it again, hanging around with all my mates – necking cheap wine and cider. I'd also just got myself a job in a bar/restaurant in town called Tonic (I started off in the kitchen when I was fifteen because I was too young for the bar), which was to become my second home. I was on the loose and I was a danger to Sunderland!

CHARLOTTE'S WORDS OF WISDOM ON: BOOZING

1. Shots are often a good idea – they have so many positives.
    *   They're a quicker way to get pissed.
    *   They're always great to toast with.
    *   They make for an amazing 'after' photo because you always pull the most ridiculous face when you've downed one (especially tequila – the slice

of lime you have afterwards makes you look like a bulldog chewing a wasp).

2. Avoid 'shit mixes' at all costs: my friends and I used to make a combination of every kind of alcohol we could find lying around the house and in the cupboards. Literally anything went in a shit mix (the clue is in the title; it tasted like shit!).

- As if it wasn't bad enough, we found that adding Baileys curdles the mixture and you feel like you're drinking actual vomit.

3. Here's a top tip for anyone like me who gets too drunk too quickly or suffers from bad hangovers: 'Vodka Water'.
   - Yes, it's really that simple, just vodka and water. Replace your usual vodka and Coke or vodka lemonade with vodka water instead! The best bit is you can't even taste the vodka! With a bit of luck by the end of the night you might still be functional enough to get home safely and remember your address.

4

ONE DARK ALLEYWAY

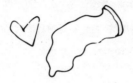

I was sixteen when I had sex for the first time. And the lucky prizewinner was a guy called Richard Waters.

The sex came pretty much straight away for me – meaning I hadn't had any initiation or build-up to the main event. There was no fingering or getting close to any other bases, no romantic lead-in or any of that stuff. Up until the fateful evening in question all I'd done was kissing (for a start I'd only just got rid of my brace and the rest of the time, as you've just heard, I'd been far too busy getting mortal to do anything else).

I wasn't the first at St Anthony's to do the deed though, no way. But it was like a peer pressure thing at our school. If you had any contact with a boy then people would be saying, 'Do you like him? Are you going to have sex?' The conversation that went round made it sound like it was as normal as having a cup of tea. The truth was, everyone was scared to do it but they just felt like they had to.

I like to think that by leaving it till I was sixteen I wasn't too bad on the easy-scale. Nevertheless, my first sexual encounter wasn't exactly *Dirty Dancing*. It was more like an episode of *Shameless*.

We didn't do it in a bed.

It didn't even happen in a house.

My first sexual experience took place on a plastic crate, down a back lane.

And I didn't have a clue what I was doing.

So to be honest, I'm not sure I can even count the deed as sex at all . . .

There was a big group of us hanging out down by Seaburn Pier drinking cider and any cheap wine we could get hold of. I'd been kissing this boy called Richard every weekend; he had blondish hair and was good-looking for our age. To this day I think he actually might be gay. Judging by my performance that night, I probably turned him. For the last few weeks everyone had been discussing whether Richard and me were going to have sex. We were the hot topic of conversation and tonight it had reached boiling point. Richard and the boys were all in a huddle talking loudly and laughing while the girls and me were in another corner, whispering and giggling. I was the talk of the pier – literally.

Every now and then, one of the lads would sidle over to where I was with the girls and say something along the lines of: 'Richard says he's going to do it with Charlotte tonight.'

All I kept thinking was: 'Where? We haven't got a bed!'

Which is why it ended up being in a back alley, on a crate.

It wasn't really what you'd call sex. We kissed for a bit and then he got his willy out, but the problem was . . . it wasn't actually hard. It was floppy! I think maybe it was all the pressure and the nerves that had built up around us (or as I said before, maybe he was gay). Either way, it was soooo awkward. We fumbled about trying to put the condom on but because his willy wasn't hard, it wasn't going on properly and all the time I was getting more nervous. It was awful! He got it in a little bit but I remember it just being very uncomfortable and feeling very cold. I reckon the whole thing must've lasted about one and a half minutes. And half of that time was taken up trying to get the condom on. After that, that same condom formed the running commentary of my life – because after our rubbish attempt at sex, we left it there on the ground in the back lane, which meant that every time anyone walked past they'd see it and shout, 'There's Charlotte's condom!'

Still, as far as I was concerned, I had HAD SEX.

I didn't do it again for a long time after that. I spent my

'intimate encounters' doing other things instead – like 'the oral'. Only problem was, I did that all wrong, too.

There was a boy called Ben Thompson. He was my first crush. I thought he looked like Brock out of Pokémon – he was really tall, dark and handsome, and had spiky hair and a chiselled jaw. He was exactly what people mean when they use the phrase 'tall, dark and handsome'. He was soooo good-looking and I fancied him more than I'd fancied anyone before. Every time I saw him I went all shy and bashful and didn't know where to look. We'd kissed a few times when we'd been drunk but I knew he thought I was a bad kisser because of that rumour that had gone round about me breaking boys' backs.

I was bad at everything (there was a theme emerging here. . .).

Which is why I have this theory: when I got older and started having lots of sex with people, I don't think of it as me being promiscuous. Instead I like to believe I was on a journey of someone trying to better themselves. Someone doing some much-needed research, someone desperate for some EXPERIENCE. Because I'd got so fed up of all the negative feedback.

Anyway, back to Ben. There was a big bush in a place called Barnes Park where everyone would go and 'do things'. Most kids would go in there and smoke bongs but I never wanted to do that. I wouldn't do drugs. But I would suck Ben Thompson's penis. Which I considered to be both safer and less illegal.

So there we were in the bush and he whipped it out. And *my oh my* it was quite big! I didn't quite know what to do. Compared to Richard's floppy friend this was a giant unicorn's horn. What I didn't realise was that some people from school, including my best friends, were spying on us. The following day a story went round the school saying, 'Charlotte was giving Ben a blow job and it fell out halfway through and there was a line of saliva from his willy to her mouth!'

Would anyone just give us a break, for God's sake?!

I was getting very sick of my life.

- I had nearly broken a boy's back from kissing him.
- There was a dirty condom in the back lane as a reminder of my first sexual encounter because it had fallen off.
- And there was now a line of saliva from my mouth to Ben Thompson's bell-end.

I needed a boyfriend who I could practise on.

CHARLOTTE'S WORDS OF WISDOM ON: SEX

Being a virgin is really in fashion at the minute – it's VERY cool. So my advice is to stay a virgin for as long as possible (if I could go back in time again that's what I'd do). But if you ARE going to have sex, then here's some stuff you might need to know:

1. Pubic hair

If you haven't slept with your potential boyfriend yet or you are single you might want to prune it. There's nothing worse than being on a night out, ending up with a boy and realising they are going to have to forage through the forest of Narnia to get to the cupboard. (However if you have a boyfriend and he doesn't accept you AND your pubes, then get rid of him!). You know someone is boyfriend material when you feel so comfortable with them that you could have a braided Mohican down there and they'd still want to have sex with you. My boyfriend Mitch has no problems with my pubes – I almost always have them unless it's a special occasion like a birthday or Valentine's.

Other times you might want to prune your pubes:

Christmas – pubes can get in the way of trying on all your new clothes you got as presents.

Holidays – it's best not to frighten the kids by the pool with your hairy spider.

Smear tests – this is an important procedure so the doctor needs full concentration, and your bush may put him or her off.

2. Vaginal farting

This is quite a common occurrence during sex (although I also like doing this as a hobby and a party trick). When it happens during the deed it can be quite embarrassing and my only bit of advice is to mask the vaginal fart with a loud cough. Several loud coughs, in fact (sometimes I just pretend

I'm choking on something – a great way of getting out of an awkward situation is with another awkward situation). Then, after he's given you the Heimlich manoeuvre, you can sexily slide into doggy style.

3. STIs

It goes without saying you MUST ALWAYS wear a condom when having sex or you will get an STI. When I was younger I got chlamydia and when I first got told I thought I was going to die. I started to plan in my head all the things I wanted to do before I left the world for good. Obviously they then explained it was something that would be completely cured with a tablet and that I still had many more years of life in me, but ever since that awful experience condoms became my best friend. I had an endless supply that were hidden in a drawer away from me mam. And never be scared to go for an STI test. My friends and me would always go for a regular check-ups if we were worried about anything or anything seemed unusual. A lot of girls we knew were too scared or embarrassed, or afraid of what people might say if they found out. All I can say is that it is so much better to be safe than sorry.

4. Anal

Look, let's not even go into this. It's just too much, too soon. I don't think we know each other well enough yet (we're only in Chapter 4, after all).

5

BOYS, BOYS, BOYS

My first ever boyfriend was called Dan Harris and I went out with him for about a year and a half. He was loads older than me which I thought was really cool – he was twenty-three and I was sixteen. Me mam and dad hated this and didn't agree with it at all. They told me I wasn't allowed to see him, so I did it on the sly.

We met at a friend's party. Dan was hard as nails and everyone was scared of him. He was the classic example of a charva – he had one of his ears pierced, always wore tracksuit bottoms and Berghaus coats and generally looked really rough. And that's why I was attracted to him – because he was so hard. Everyone knew not to mess with him; he'd been stabbed in fights and everything. What's more, he wanted to go out with ME.

We were all at a house party one night and we'd started chatting and having a laugh. I was doing my research at that time so it wasn't long before we were kissing and even less time before we were upstairs having sex (fuelled by a lot of cider and Lambrini).

I'd got a bit of practice in since my disastrous encounter with Richard so I was definitely a bit better at it this time. But I remember being embarrassed because Dan was older than me and I was still convinced he'd think I was rubbish and wouldn't ever want to see me again.

But the next day he rang me.

'Charlotte, we're all going out tonight if you want to come?'

I was in shock. I was elated! But . . . here's where it gets tricky . . . I was also on my period. And me being *me* decided – for some unknown reason – that I needed to tell him.

'Well, I'm on my period.'

That literally was the first thing I said to him on the phone! How *embarrassing*. I remember I was in the Spar at the time buying some Cheese Strings and snacks to go to my mates because we were going to watch a Disney film. What a contrast! I'm young enough to be watching cartoons yet here I was trying to explain to a twenty-three-year-old man that he probably wouldn't be able to have sex with me because I was on my PERIOD.

That's fucked up.

Then Dan dropped the bombshell that made me fall in love with him instantly.

'Charlotte – that's not the only reason I want you to come out, you know!'

So he became my boyfriend. Well, once he'd finished with his other *girlfriend*, that was. I should've realised there and then that he was going to be bad news. If a man cheats on someone else by seeing you – sooner or later *you'll* be the one being cheated on.

We were together for about a year and we argued *all* the time. I knew he was cheating on me because he would constantly have suckies on his neck (he'd try telling me they were from his friends who'd been messing about!). The problem was, I'd really fallen for him. He was the first of many fellas I would find it very hard to get over.

But in the end there was no option but to finish things because Dan started getting a bit violent towards me. He would wait for me in the back lane near the house where I'd walk to get the bus and he'd shout at me and push me about. Typically, after all the cheating *he'd* been doing, *he* was the one who ended up getting eaten up by paranoia! He was convinced his friends were flirting with me and that I fancied one of them. He'd constantly be having a go at me but the only time he properly scared me was when he threatened to come to my house and smash my windows in. And I couldn't have anything affecting my family. So that was the end of him.

After Dan I met my next boyfriend: Alex.

My friends *hated* Alex. But I was blind to his cheating ways.

Alex was a footballer and played for Bradford on the reserves team and was VERY good-looking. He used to live away in the week and then come back at weekends. We met on Facebook and one night he came to pick me up in his car.

Alex had a little silver Corsa and it was a big deal. I'd never met anyone with his own set of wheels before. We'd drive to a certain spot and pull up in a back lane amongst the fields where there's an amazing view of Sunderland. And we'd buy food from the shop so we could have snacks while we were there.

At the beginning we had such a laugh together – he even took me on holiday for my eighteenth birthday. We went to Costa del Sol – and our mams took us to the airport (we were so unworldly – we didn't have a clue how to get through Security; it was like we thought we were on an alien spacecraft or something. Our parents were cracking up watching us). Up until now, if I'm honest, I hadn't really enjoyed sex all that much, but with Alex I started to like it. I started experimenting and I'd go to Ann Summers and get sexy outfits. I thought I was porn star material!

But as my friends had tried to warn me all along, Alex was bad news. He was cheating on me. I think there are some men who just can't help it. It's like it's in their genes or something. I heard loads of rumours and at first I didn't want to listen. But eventually I knew it had to end. And obviously it wasn't going to end well.

I was so angry I keyed his car. Then I ran him over (well, I drove past him and accidentally clipped the side of his leg then he walked off. I don't think he would've counted it as being run over).

He definitely saw the full force of Psycho Charlotte! I was such a pest, calling his house in the night, threatening him . . . his mam and dad *hated* me. I'd see him out in clubs and if he was talking to other girls I'd run over and throw my drink on him. I remember hiding behind walls and spying on him like a quivering mess. Then I'd swill him with booze (what a waste!).

Then I met Kevin Harper. He was the love of my life (at the time anyway) and unlike all the others he never cheated on me. He was my first toy boy – he was seventeen and I was nineteen and his body was *amazing* (A.MAZING) because he was an MMA fighter. We added each other on Facebook after being introduced by my best friend Anna and started phoning each other and chatting for hours. I'd never spoken to a boy like that before; we'd talk about loads of random things just like I did with my mates. I was his first proper girlfriend and we were together for over a year. He'd come and see me every day after he'd finished training and we'd have dinner together and in the winter we'd build igloos in the snow (our main big fight was over the fact that he once built an igloo with his mates instead of with me). We'd sit in and watch telly with a Chinese takeaway – which sometimes meant he wouldn't make his weight in training and his dad would go mad at him.

Then one dark evil night, he told me he didn't want to see me any more. He didn't love me, he said. I think he'd grown apart from me and just saw me as a friend. I was sat on the edge of his bed as he was trying to break the news and I could see in his eyes he didn't want to hurt me, that's what made the whole thing more painful – I couldn't go mad at him like I did with my other boyfriends because I knew he wasn't a bad person. But I couldn't understand how he could just suddenly stop loving me. He kept saying, 'I'm so sorry,' and he looked like he wanted to cry. For the next few weeks I was devastated. Inconsolable. I can't remember feeling pain like it; it was as if someone had died. I felt like someone had removed something from my chest, I had this constant anxious feeling, numb and empty. I'd ring and ring his phone but he wouldn't answer. I left voicemails in tears.

Even though we'd ended, I still had a key to his house (I don't know how I ever had one in the first place, if I'm honest) and I kept calling him because I wanted to see him.

One night after I'd been out on the town with my mates, I rang and asked him where he was – he said he was at his friend's house but I didn't believe him. I thought he was just saying it so I wouldn't go round to his. So I thought, 'I'm just going to go and let myself in.' So I went to my bedroom, got the key out of my drawer, got a taxi to his house, let myself in, went upstairs, took my dress off and got into his bed in my underwear.

Suddenly I heard a familiar voice. 'Charlotte? What are you doing?'

'Oh . . . Hi, Nigel.'

I was in bed with his dad.

It turns out his dad snores, so if Kevin were ever out his mam would make him sleep in Kevin's bed so she could get some sleep.

I immediately phoned home. 'Mam! Come and pick me up – I'm in bed with Kevin's dad!'

After that I left a voicemail on Kevin's phone: 'I've done a bad thing . . . I got in bed with your dad.'

Kevin rang me back immediately (he hadn't responded to any of my other voicemails quite so speedily). 'What happened? I can't go home in case Mam and Dad are angry!'

'Well, think how I feel! You didn't get into bed with one of them.'

Boyfriend break-ups were the worst. Each time one happened I'd get myself into the same messed-up, feeling miserable and sorry for myself routine. Every morning at 3 a.m. I'd run the bath, get in and sit there, wailing and waking up the whole house. Mam says it was like having a baby and I'd go through the same pattern and process every time – I couldn't settle for about three months, then all of a sudden I'd be over it. Mam would sit stroking my hair saying, 'Charlotte, it's not the end of the world. Time will go by and you'll forget all this, I promise.' I didn't believe it at the time but now I know mams are *always right*.

Well, nearly always.

6

'DAAAD, I'VE CRASHED THE CAR'

The day I smashed up my car. As remembered by me dad, Gary Crosby . . .

Charlotte's first car was a brand-new black Corsa; it was a lovely little motor. She'd just got through the first year of insurance and we were celebrating her having a no-claims bonus. That was until we got a phone call early one Sunday morning – her mam, Letitia, and I were still in bed. Charlotte had been out with her mates the night before, and was driving. Here's how the conversation went:

Charlotte: 'Daaad, I've got something to tell you, do you promise not to be angry?'

Me: 'What?'

Charlotte: 'Do you promise?'

Me: 'Have you been arrested?'

Charlotte: 'No, nothing that bad . . .'

Me: 'Well?'

Charlotte: 'I have had a little crash in the car . . .'

Me: 'Are you OK?'

Charlotte: 'Yeah, I'm fine . . .'

Me: 'How is the car?'

Charlotte: 'Well, I don't think it's that bad, but Christina's mam thinks it's a write-off.'

Me: 'Eh? A write-off? Are you sure you're not hurt?'

Charlotte: 'Oh no, I'm fine. But Laura has a dislocated shoulder, Christina was knocked unconscious and the boys took themselves to hospital.' Me: (putting phone down): 'I'm on my way . . .'

I drove to Christina's mam's where Charlotte had stayed the night and saw the car. It was shaped like a banana! There was no doubt it was a write-off. I somehow managed to drive it home but as I did it kept trying to turn into the kerb because the whole thing was shaped like a boomerang.

When I questioned Charlotte afterwards, she told me they were all singing out loud to some daft song and she went around a roundabout too fast and nearly rolled over. She'd rolled over all right – onto the roundabout, which only a few weeks ago had been fitted with a floral display – it was so pretty it had won a council flower award. Most of the flowers ended up on Charlotte's car – I could hardly see through the windscreen as I was driving it home.

The next day her granddad came to see us knowing nothing about the car crash. As he walked into the house, he said, 'You'll never guess what! You know those brand-new tall flower stands that have just been erected on Durham Road this week? Some horrible little scumbag has demolished one of them, the flowers are all over the road – what a mess!'

Turns out, the only thing that had prevented the car from doing a full rollover was this brand-new five-foot tall flowerbed arrangement, an array of round trays on top of each other. Had it not been for this council-funded flowerbed, the girls would all have been killed. Although I don't think they were intended as a crash barrier! The council didn't replace the display for months and all that was left was the small pole that had held the flowerbeds together. Every time we drove past we would say, 'Aye, there's that flowerbed where Charlotte tried to kill herself!'

The car was written off and we had to pay the loan off. Her insurance went through the roof and we ended up getting her a cheap little Beetle. We were really disappointed, but it could have been a lot worse.

After I passed my driving test (it might be hard to believe but I passed first time!), I started to take my car *everywhere*. It felt so liberating not to have to rely on parents to take us to places and we hardly ever had money for taxis – so I became 'Charlotte the taxi driver'. This came in especially handy when there were boys going out whom we fancied – because it meant we could follow them. That night, I hadn't had a drink, I'd just had water. When I was driving I would offer the boys a lift home but, because there were so many of them, someone would normally have to go in the boot.

Thank God we all had our seatbelts on the night of the crash. I remember we were listening to 'Don't Stop Me Now' by Queen and it was raining. I clearly thought I was Lewis Hamilton and started showing off and messing about with the wheel. I was moving it about really quickly, like I was a snake – but I lost control and we skidded everywhere. Suddenly we were on the roundabout and the car was sliding about on the grassy verge, going round and round really fast, and everyone was screaming. Then I crashed into the flower display and one of the windows smashed to smithereens.

When the car finally came to a halt I turned round and saw all my friends with their heads bowed down. Were they OK? Had I killed them?!

I was in the front with Tom, a boy I fancied at the time, and I was screaming at him, 'They're dead!' I didn't know what to do. He started shaking them and we could see Laura's tongue was bleeding. She came to and kept saying, 'My nose! It's broken!' She was delirious because it wasn't even her nose, I think it was her shoulder that she hurt but she was shouting and wailing and I couldn't calm her down. Anna woke up and shrieked, 'I can't move my arm,' then Christina lay there for ages before she opened her eyes and started moaning in pain: 'Owwww!'

Everyone was alive – thank God – but they could hardly move.

'Is the car driveable?'

'I don't know!'

'Try it! We have to get out of here!'

We were on the roundabout and it was about 2.30 a.m. The car was making this creaky noise like it was in pain too. Somehow I started to drive off the roundabout with the bonnet and the roof covered in flowers – we looked like something at a festival. I dropped the others off, parked outside Christina's house and slept in her room. There's no way I could take it home.

The next morning, when I rang me dad, my heart was beating. I was so scared he was going to go mad. But he was more worried about whether I was injured. Being a parent can't be easy – and definitely not being one to me!

By this time me mam and dad were also parents to my brother Nathaniel (I'm fifteen years older than him, he's ten now). When me mam first told me she was pregnant I was so angry! I'd got used to being an only child and wanted Mam and Dad all to myself. I didn't like the thought of having a brother; I liked being an only child because it meant I got all the attention. But thank God she never listened to me because I love Nathaniel to bits.

Nathaniel was born on 11 October 2004 and he weighed a massive 10 pounds 2 ounces. Well, what can you expect when you have a dad who's 6 foot 4 inches? Me poor mam had to have a lot of stitches in her vagina afterwards – Nathaniel was so long he'd split her in half.

I felt weird holding him at first because he had all this dark hair like a little rat. But it wasn't long before we developed a bond and he became like my little plaything. Once he started to get cuter, I decided he was ready for me to take him into town in the pram.

It always looked really trendy if you had a pram. It was the 'in thing'. If you knew someone who had a baby you'd always want to be allowed to take it out on a Saturday. It was considered really cool. Now I think about it, it's so backwards. Why is walking around town pretending you have a baby aged fifteen anything to show off about?!

As our bond grew and he got even cuter, I started to love him even more. It wasn't until he got to the age of about three that we started to notice that he was really *really* intelligent. He'd already started talking way earlier than any of the other kids, but it was as his conversation grew that we began to notice he was different. While other kids would talk about basic stuff like food and toys, Nathaniel had an *obsession* with cars. By the age of four he could identify every make of every different kind of car and knew where each vehicle came from. He'd go for walks with me dad and point out each car he came across – telling us the exact make and model! At first we thought he was just going to be some kind of car fanatic but it wasn't just cars. As each year passed he'd start getting obsessed with something different. When he was six he was into countries and flags and started to be able to name every single one of them at a glance.

He also loved going on the computer but every time he did he'd push his face really close to the screen. Then one day my phone started ringing – it was me mam and she was crying her eyes out.

'What's wrong?'

'It's Nathaniel.'

'Is he OK?' (Me mam always overreacts about everything, she gets *very* emotional.)

'He's nearly blind in one eye! We've just been to the doctor and he's got bad sight. He's needed glasses for so long and none of us knew!' She was hysterical by now.

'Calm down, Mam! It's not bad that he needs glasses!'

All I can think is that because I'd been so healthy, she felt guilty for not noticing. Like any sane person, I just told her to go and get him some glasses. 'He won't mind he didn't get them earlier, it's not like he's been crying about it or has been in any pain.'

I'll never forget the day we went to get him some specs. As he walked out of the optician he kept staring at the pavement in awe. 'Wow! Wow!' he was saying and studying the floor like it was the most beautiful thing in the world. 'All the lines in the pavement are so clear!' he laughed. It was the cutest thing ever. He'd finally started to see everything properly!

It was only when he began school that the teachers started noticing his behaviour was different to the other kids. He would shy away at playtimes and stand against the wall, not speaking to anyone. He would literally push his face right up against the wall for the duration of playtime. His glasses were constantly scratched – all because he was trying to hug the wall. At first, me mam and dad just thought he was really shy – but then it didn't make sense because he wasn't at all shy at home. So the teachers sent him to have these different social tests and the result came back that he was on the autism spectrum and he had Asperger's. The tests showed that he didn't feel comfortable in social situations, he didn't like being around other children – in fact, he couldn't stand it. Still, to this day, when he's around his own age group he doesn't know what to say or how to behave and he's only really got one friend at school. He gets invited to two birthday parties a year which means we have to make a massive effort and we all go with him. He still goes a bit weird when he's there but at least he's stopped hugging the wall now!

He also stopped going out at playtime and prefers to stay inside with the teachers. He never gets picked on, though; he's a very happy kid and always comes home with funny stories about this girl who's dead naughty and everyone laughs at her. I'm positive he would tell us if he was getting singled out. And when he's around older people he's in his element. He can socialise better with adults than he can with younger people – so me mam and dad have to take him away when it's not the school holidays because if he goes somewhere and there are loads of kids about he can't relax, he will just sit on the sunbed and won't move. It's as if he's terrified to even go in the pool and its horrible to see.

I was quite ignorant about Asperger's to start with, mainly because I didn't understand it. So when Nathaniel was being naughty or acting unusually and I saw me mam being nice to him I'd say, 'Mam he's just acting up! You shouldn't be doing this, you need to be more harsh on him!' and she would try to reason with me: 'Charlotte, he's got autism, you can't do that, you have to act differently with him.'

I thought I should treat him like every other child. Whereas now I've grown up with Asperger's I know the little things he does and how the condition makes him act. For example, if you're going to go somewhere or if something's changing in the house, you need to warn him weeks before. If you say, 'Right, Nathaniel, we're off to the shops now, come on!' then he doesn't know what to do and starts to get frustrated. He actually knows more about his condition than me, though – there are books that are written by kids with autism and they explain exactly how they feel and why they feel it. Nathaniel has one and he's read it over and over again and now knows *everything* to the point that sometimes I think he uses it to his advantage! We'll be arguing and all of a sudden he'll shout out, 'Mam! Charlotte isn't taking into account me AS,' – he calls it AS because that's what the book calls it – 'and she's not understanding that it's making me feel a certain way!' So I get told off and then I think, 'Why did we ever give him that book?!' He's still super intelligent but, these days, he's more into computer games than cars or flags. All of his focus and time goes into playing people online in America and around the world. And he *always* beats them because he's really clever.

It's never a problem that my brother has Asperger's. He's not very high on the autism spectrum so it's not as notice-able as it might be with some kids. He's just weird in different ways – and, to be honest, I was a bit weird at school so what's the difference?

7

'I'M GOING TO JUMP!'

As Nathaniel was growing up into a loving, caring, amazing child, I was busy boozing, partying with my mates, dating boys and waking up me mam and dad at all hours of the night because I needed a lift home from a bush somewhere. I'd regularly get so drunk that my friends would ring to tell them I was unconscious on the floor somewhere and they'd have to come and pick me up. Either that or I'd get in from a night out and I'd wake everyone up because I'd be running around the house, making phone calls or late-night toasted sandwiches.

Then of course there was what's come to be known in our family as 'the roof incident'. It happened when I was eighteen or nineteen, back when I was dating Alex (remember him from page 46?). It was a typical night in our relationship – we'd gone out and I'd lost him, and when I called to see where he was he wasn't answering his phone (the cheat!). So I got home from my night out, a girl on a mission, psychotically *obsessed* with tracking him down at all costs. I was calling him and leaving angry messages on his answerphone – shouting into the receiver really loudly with absolutely no consideration for the fact that it was about three in the morning and everyone else in the house was trying to sleep. I was being so noisy that everyone had woken up and me mam was not happy.

The next thing I know, Mam and me are on the floor – wrestling! – and Dad's trying to tear us apart. I'm shouting, 'Get the police, I'm pressing assault charges on her!' While Dad is standing there saying, 'Don't be so stupid.'

'I knew you'd take her side!' I hollered.

Dad was mad and took my phone off me. I was so pissed and angry I just saw red and the next minute I was holding onto his ankles, biting them. As he tried to walk back to his room he was dragging me along the floor, nipping at his heels in an attempt to get my phone back.

Eventually Dad picked me up, put me in my room and shut the door. He and Mam got back into their bed. That's when they heard a window open and shut.

'She's going on the bloody roof!'

Yep, I'd climbed onto the roof of the house in protest. I think I even threatened to commit suicide unless I got the phone back! Obviously I would never do that in a million years, but they didn't know that.

'Come down, Charlotte! What about the neighbours?'

'Fuck the neighbours!'

Next thing I remember is waking up in bed with me mam, and dad. Turns out I'd been out on the roof for so long that I fell asleep up there and Mam had called the police.

Here's how me dad, Gary Crosby, remembers it:

It was a typical Saturday night in the summer of 2010. Charlotte had gone out with her friends into Sunderland. Myself, Letitia and Nathaniel had a normal night in and went to bed around 11 p.m. We have given Charlotte about half a dozen sets of keys over the years but they regularly go missing. I went through a stage where I'd changed the front door lock three times in the same month; I'd changed it so often that when I went back to B&Q for the third time I noticed I was still the most recent customer as I recognised the damaged packaging on the next lock. I became an expert locksmith thanks to Charlotte losing keys. Often they would randomly reappear inside a shoe or under the tree in the front garden, by which time the locks had been changed anyway.

So, there we are, tucked up in bed. At about 3 a.m. we hear a taxi outside, the chime of the doorbell follows and then there's shouting through the letterbox – something about having no key (this is standard drunken chat on a return home). Letitia goes downstairs and opens the door and Charlotte literally falls into the hallway – she is beyond 'mortal', completely hammered and in a foul mood. She starts ranting about how her boyfriend has been ignoring her and how, to top it all, she'd got lost. She has actually come home to get more money and thinks she's going back out. It's 3 a.m! Letitia gets into an argument with her about how stupid it is to go back out and that no taxi would take her. They struggle. This continues into the bedroom and I have finally heard enough; I go into bedroom to find Letitia dragging Charlotte by the feet towards her bed. This progresses to a full-on wrestle with hair pulling. I intervene and split them apart. Letitia is crying, Charlotte is completely blitzed, starry-eyed and incoherent.

Letitia: 'She is out of control, she's going back out again, but look at the state of her!'

Charlotte: 'I want to press charges against her, I have been assaulted!'

Me: 'Don't be daft. Christ almighty, go to bed. You are so pissed!'

Charlotte: 'I knew you would side with her!' (She starts becoming hysterical.)

We both lift her and put her into bed. She starts ranting about never being so humiliated in her life and that her parents don't love her. Only her boyfriend understands her and she must go and see him. She must see him THIS MINUTE.

Me: 'It's now 3.30 a.m., where you going to go at this time? Everyone is in bed.'

Charlotte: 'You are thick, you know nothing!'

Cue a tirade of abuse at both of us. We're speechless and I snap.

Me: 'OK, I will have this phone and I will take this purse and I will have these house keys! I am going to bed: you are going nowhere, girl.'

I take her purse, keys and phone and try to walk out of the room. She grabs hold of my ankles and I end up dragging her across the laminate floor for ten feet like a limp sausage until finally she loses her grip.

I give her a lecture but she is now almost unconscious. We both reckon she will fall asleep. We leave her in her room; she is slumped on the bed, fully clothed. We get back into our bed.

Five minutes later we hear a noise. It's a window, there are things getting knocked over, it sounds like there's someone outside. What?!

Letitia goes to check and runs back into our room.

Letitia: 'She's on the bloody roof!'

Charlotte's room is above a garage and there is a small sloping roof in front of her window, a ledge of about a metre in width, sloping above the garage. Below that, there's a ten-foot drop to ground. I spring up, put some clothes on and dash outside. She is perched on the roof like a bird ready to jump . . . but not quite sure whether her wings will work. It's a pathetic sight. Her hair is a mess from the fight, her makeup has run down her face and her eyes are heavy from the alcohol. She is a real mess. I start thinking, 'Health and safety alert – she could fall!' I talk to her calmly, trying to get her to go back in the room.

Me: 'Charlotte, please, this is silly, you could hurt yourself. Climb back in the bedroom.'

Charlotte: 'You are an idiot, I have been beaten up in my own room, I am going back out and you cannot stop me.'

Cue further hysterical rantings, most of which are about how she is disgusted with her parents as they are 'so unfair'. Think Kevin and Perry in full effect.

Me: 'You are making a right scene now, keep your voice down, all of the neighbours are in bed!'

Charlotte (at the top of her voice): 'I don't care about the neighbours! They are all idiots too!' (Screams) 'YOU ARE ALL IDIOTS, EVERY ONE OF YOU IN YOUR BEDS, ID-I-OTS ID-I-OTS! III-DDD-III-OOO-TTT-SSSS! YOU ARE ALL A BUNCH OF IDIOTS!' (She repeats this in the style of an insane out-of-tune football chant.)

This has clearly got out of control; our daughter is out of it. I am desperate. I go into the garage to get a ladder. I am going to have to climb up and get her. It's now 4 a.m! She is still rambling about going back out – it's nearly sunrise. I get the stepladder and climb up. She is crying, ranting, murmuring and incoherent. She seems a bit remorseful, so I give her the nice guy act – when all I really want to do is pull her off the roof and give her good bloody kick up the a**e. But she is a young girl and it wouldn't look good. By now the curtains are twitching and lights have come on around the street.

Me (taking a deep breath): 'Look, you know we love you, we will do anything for you, you make us so proud, but it's really late and all your friends will be in bed.'

She doesn't look up. Her voice has stopped, her head is in her arms, face buried, and she's fallen silent.

Me: 'We can sort this all out tomorrow, I will drive you where you want in the morning . . .'

I ramble on for about five minutes. She's still silent, not moving, and she's starting to breathe deeply. Bloody hell, I have bored her to sleep! She is flat out, unconscious, sitting on the roof with her legs tucked up to her chest, her face buried onto her arms, which are folded across her knees. She hasn't heard a single word of my Nice Father routine, or if she has she was so unimpressed it sent her drifting off.

Now what am I going to do? I can't wake her up! I shake her but she is out for the count – and then she starts snoring. It's a sloping roof so I can't just leave her; she could fall off and crack her skull. It's now 4.30 a.m. and the birds are tweeting.

When she was little I could easily carry her to bed, but she's now a full-grown adult and I have been skipping the gym in the last few years. I am not as fit as I used to be.

I take a deep breath and summon all of my strength, psyching myself up like a great Olympian weight lifter . . . and with a big heave she is over my shoulder. The stepladder groans and shakes uncontrollably; it's not meant for two people – and definitely not a dead-weight drunk. I move each leg down the steps; each step requires a herculean effort. She is fast asleep, doesn't make a sound. I get to the bottom and stagger towards the front door. Letitia is standing there, not sure whether to laugh or cry, 'Clear the route, I'm coming through.'

67

Suddenly there are voices behind me; two police officers are standing there.

'What's going on 'ere then?' one of them says.

Letitia starts telling them but I need to get this drunken weight off my back so I plough on up the stairs. Eventually I manage to plop her on her bed. She hasn't twitched. I am exhausted, dripping in sweat and aching all over. The police come into the room and check her, and me. I look like I'm having a heart attack. We chat downstairs and have a bit of a laugh about it all, they leave and we go off to bed. It's now 5 a.m. We are shattered. Charlotte is in the Land of Nod, blissfully snoring away.

The next day, Charlotte remembers nothing, absolutely zero. She starts crying, saying she can't believe she did that and that she is so sorry for what she has done. We laugh it off in the morning, especially when we recall how my Mr Nice Guy chat sent her to sleep!

Just another normal weekend in Charlotte's world . . .

What have I done to deserve such brilliant parents? No matter what I seemed to throw at them, they'd always end up laughing about it eventually. Most of my mates' parents were dead strict so they'd be really jealous of me mam and dad. When I think about all the things I've done – coming home so mortal, shouting abuse at them, climbing onto roofs, crashing cars – I realise how lucky I am. It also meant I would never lie to them because I didn't have to; they always said they'd rather I woke them up in the middle of

the night asking for a lift home than get lost somewhere or end up with a random stranger.

CHARLOTTE'S WORDS OF WISDOM ON: HAVING AN AMAZING NIGHT OUT ON A BUDGET

Pre-drinking – Getting a little bit tipsy before you go out means you can skip buying the expensive drinks in the first bar.

Get the bus/walk/get a lift off a mate/Mam or Dad – It is your parents' duty after all, so tell them *they* chose to have a child so *they* have to deal with the consequences. Getting a lift is a good way to minimise the costs of getting a taxi both ways. BUT YOU DO NEED TO GET A TAXI HOME IF NO ONE CAN PICK YOU UP: it is not safe to go walking home in the early hours of the morning and it gets cold.

Share drinks – Instead of each of you all buying separate drinks, buy a jug to share or a larger drink to share. It's both cheaper and takes you a bit longer to get drunk.

Get in the club for free – I would always flutter my eyes! Or try to get a boy I fancied to pay for me to get in. Another great one is to pretend you've lost your friends and you have no money and ask if they could just let you in 'real quick' to see if you can find them. Then when you're in there, run and hide!

Share a cab home – Always stick with the people you went out with so that on the way home you can all share a taxi (and the fare).

Even though Mam and Dad would laugh and joke about what I'd put them through, they weren't pushovers. When it came to my GCSEs they made me stay in every weekend for six weeks and do two hours of revision every night after school. I was in the bottom sets at school but they were determined for me to do as well as I could. I'd get home and they'd start the clock – 'Right, 6 p.m., time to sit down!' – and only after I'd put the hours in revising would I be able to go out and see my mates. Immediately after I'd taken my exams I was convinced that I'd failed and was trying to think of excuses to tell me mam. But then I passed (most of them anyway) and I was on top of the world. But to this day I still think it's better to tell yourself something's going to be bad . . . that way, when something good *does* happen it's more of a surprise. And you can never be disappointed if you have low expectations, can you?

Here's what I got in my GCSEs:

Graphic Design: C

PE: C

Maths: C

Science: C

History: G

Well, I didn't know anything about old stuff and I hated the history teacher, Mrs Gordon.

Spanish: F

RE: B

I didn't really need to revise for RE because I know everything about God. For starters, I know that God isn't a person because when you say 'In the name of the Father, the Son and the Holy Spirit', God is actually supposed to be *all three* of those! Complex, right? I used to think He was actually just a person who lives in the clouds but He's *everywhere* and can be *everything*. I actually think I'm quite a religious person. I used to pray when I was younger – to get more pocket money. And one of my dad's friends was poorly so I prayed for him, too. I used to always pray that my family would be OK – my nana was getting older and I hated the idea of death so I'd always pray that no one would die. I haven't prayed for a long time, though.

English: D

I wasn't very good at English but it was very important to make sure you had good handwriting at school. I used to practise my writing in the summer holidays. All the popular girls would have really nice handwriting. There would be the long, wide writing, the sharp, tall, thin writing and there would be the one with the bubbly shaped 'a'. If you wrote your letter 'a' like that then you were popular.

I'd always start like that and forget half way through, though.

After my GCSEs I wanted to go to Sixth Form because that's what all my mates were doing. I didn't have a clue what I wanted to do so I just copied them. I chose all the same subjects as them – Business, IT and RE. Somehow or other I'd managed to get a B in RE at GCSE. But taking courses at A level just because I wanted to be in the same classes as my mates was the stupidest thing I've ever done. I didn't even like them! (The subjects, not my mates.)

I loved Sixth Form, though. It was so laid back! You'd have gaps between lessons where you could sit in the common room with your mates and eat or do nothing. You'd be able to walk outside for dinner (without getting chased by Bulldog) and you could do anything you wanted – there was so much freedom. Which, to me, meant freedom to mess about!

Natalie and me would spend most of the time making funny videos – we'd miss lessons because we were messing about so much. We'd make stupid videos of Steve Irwin – Natalie would be Steve because she could do his accent and I'd be a crocodile trying to attack her. Or we'd pretend to be zombies in the locker room and scare people as they were coming in. We were so immature. We were constantly messing around and I thought, 'This is what I want to do! Why can't you just be silly and get paid for it?'

I suppose in a way it came true.

I lasted in Sixth Form for a year . . . until a 'fight' forced me to leave.

It was on a night out one weekend; we'd been knocking about with a different group of girls. One of them was called Holly and she was friends with my boyfriend at the time. It was a typical drunken night and I was kicking off about something my boyfriend had done. I was ranting and I threw a glass and it smashed. Holly came over, trying to help me, and was saying, 'Charlotte are you OK?' but she was doing it in a really annoying way like she didn't mean it. I was pissed out of my head and angry at the world and somehow ended up lashing out at her. We rolled around on the floor like a pair of old washerwomen having a brawl. I was so out of it.

Despite the incomprehensible state I was in, I knew I'd done something bad and I went to bed that night thinking, 'What have I done?'

Now, if it had been one of my friends from my normal group and I'd had a fight in a drunken rage, they'd have been slightly mad but would have forgiven me because they'd have known I didn't mean it. But Holly wasn't one of my normal friends. And she certainly wasn't going to let me forget about what I'd done.

Instead, she got the police involved.

I'd already told Mam and Dad I'd had a bit of a fight but that it was no big deal. A couple of days later, though, Dad was in the garage and the police turned up. 'We need to speak to your daughter, Charlotte.'

I was taken to the police station and informed that her parents wanted to press charges. Holly had told the police that she had horrendous injuries from our fight so we were both asked to give statements about what had happened. It was so scary, I was full of anxiety – everyone has fights when they're teenagers but I knew I'd gone too far and I was really worried I'd get a criminal record.

I went back to Sixth Form and Holly rocked up with this massive black eye. I wasn't really the fighting type (mortal drunk, yes, but I wasn't someone who hurt people). I was made to feel a real bully and people started looking at me weirdly and treating me differently after that. So I ended up leaving Sixth Form because I felt so bad and couldn't handle the hassle I was getting.

I wasn't exactly blowing the teachers away with my knowledge of Business and IT anyway.

Thankfully, in the end, the police thought it was all overblown. Despite Holly claiming to have suffered all these horrendous injuries, the hospital records said there were hardly any marks on her. And when she got her mate involved as a witness, neither of their stories matched.

Phew! I was off the hook.

Mam wasn't going to forget it in a hurry, though. 'You *ever* dare get into another fight!'

CHARLOTTE'S WORDS OF WISDOM ON: BEING A TEENAGER

Your teenage years have got to be the most dramatic! Everything's going on:

- You're getting pubes
- You're starting periods
- You fancy boys (or in a boy's case, your balls are dropping and you've probably started wanking)
- You're kicking off and getting angry about everything.
- You find you're in for a bumpy ride with your parents as you start to realise they are really uncool (well, mine were)
- You discover alcohol and going out
- You make mistakes but learn a lot

Your teenage years are all about:

Living, loving, laughing so hard you pee your pants, making amazing memories, breaking the rules, dreaming big and being completely carefree.

All I can ultimately say is: ENJOY EVERY MOMENT OF THESE YEARS BECAUSE THEY FLY SO FAST! I wish I could do mine all over again x 1000.

8

'MAM... IT'S ME, CHARLOTTE...'

According to me mam, from the minute I turned sixteen it was as if I'd metamorphosed into a different person. Personally I thought I was the same person all along but the way she describes it, it's as if I'd changed from a hamster to a werewolf. 'You're not normal!' she would say to me, rolling her eyes. I was always getting myself into some sort of trouble but because I usually ended up in a stupid situation, me mam and dad spent more time laughing at me than being angry with me.

Mam says it's because I don't have any boundaries. She

says I never think, 'Oh, I won't do that because I'll get told off.' She reckons that if I want to do it I'll do it, no matter what the consequences. Dad, on the other hand, says he just thinks I have psychopathic tendencies.

No matter how much I got punished it never made a remote bit of difference to what I'd do next. What's that saying? 'You learn from your mistakes'? Well, I never did.

One day, Dad took my car keys off me and confiscated my car as a punishment. So what did I do? I stole the car back again!

I can't remember what I'd done wrong this time but I was obviously playing up enough for Dad to decide he was taking my car away from me – 'No car for a week!' – he said and he drove it to his mam's house, Nana Doreen, for safe-keeping.

Well, I wasn't having any of that. I thought, 'I'm sick of this!' So I immediately said to one of my mates, 'I've got my spare key – let's go and steal it back from me dad!' My friend drove to me nana's house and we cunningly parked out of sight, up the street. It was like we were on some sleuth undercover army operation – I was dressed in camou-flaged clothes and everything. I could see me dad and me brother Nathaniel through the window in me nana's house, so I carefully slunk down onto the driveway and crawled along on my front so no one would see me – it was like *Bear Grylls: Mission Survive*. I opened the car door and eased myself carefully into the driver's seat, keeping a beady eye on the window to ensure my punisher hadn't clocked me. The problem was, because my six-foot four-inch dad had literally just been in the vehicle, the seat was pushed so far back that I could barely touch the pedals. My heart was in my mouth, it was pounding so fast, and my fingers were trembling as I put my key in the ignition. I pushed my foot on the accelerator so hard I went doughnutting out of the drive and sped off down the road like the car in *Back to the Future*. All I could see were me dad, me nana and Nathaniel's shocked faces pressed up against the window as I flew past them like a speck of dust. A bit of me felt guilty and thought, 'Charlotte, you can't do this. You're leaving your dad and your little brother stranded!' (Nathaniel was only about two at the time and our house was about half an hour away from my nana's.)

But then I realised I was victorious. I'd done it – I'd stolen the car back! That's when I went missing from home for two weeks. As soon as I'd taken the car I knew I was in big trouble and didn't want to face the consequences!

After my undercover car rescue mission outside Nana Doreen's, I went to Anna's house where I spent most of my runaway time until Anna's mam said, 'Charlotte can't stay here any more, she's been here every night!' So then I went to Laura's until her mam got fed up of me too. Then I went to Christina's and after I'd exhausted her hospitality, I found a parking spot about six minutes' drive away from me mam and dad's house and stopped there for a few nights, sleeping in the front with the seat reclined all the way back. I'd borrowed a quilt from Anna and had snuck back home to get some clothes when I knew me mam and dad were out. Until one night a policeman found me. Someone must have reported the fact that the same car had been parking in the same spot every night; it must've been logged as 'suspicious behaviour'. I heard a knock on my window.

'What are you doing here, young lady?'

I didn't know what to say, I was a bit embarrassed.

'Oh, I had nowhere to stay so I've been sleeping in me car, officer.'

I was scared I might get locked up. But he just looked at me as if I was a bit odd.

'Oh, right, OK.'

And then he walked off.

Mam, meanwhile, was frantic. Every day she'd be on the phone to one of my friends and at first she was just shouting all the time: 'Charlotte is absolutely out of order for stealing the car! Her brother and her dad were stranded, I had to go and pick them up and I had work the next day!' but before long her mood changed from really angry to crying and begging someone to put me on the phone. 'Can we just get her back? Tell Charlotte to come home! Please!'

I refused to speak to her but she knew I was safe.

During this time I was working at a bar called Tonic (I *loved* it at Tonic – but more of that later) and I'd made friends with a boy called Dan who worked on the bar. He had big ginger hair, was dead skinny like a stick, really pale and covered in tattoos. I'd never seen anyone who looked

Me playing the Big Brother board game... it was written in the stars.

Me, mam and dad. Mam dressed me – I look horrendous!

Looking all cute and innocent for once.

Me, mam and dad chilling at home.

Left: Rocking the school uniform. Best days of my life.

Bottom: Me and my homosexual rabbit.

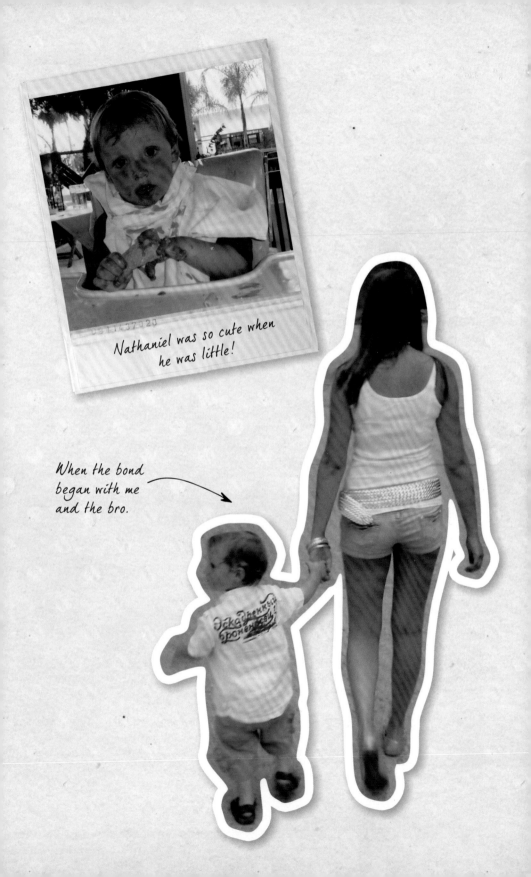

Nathaniel was so cute when he was little!

When the bond began with me and the bro.

Me and Nathaniel went through a stage where we were a bit ugly!

But we soon grew out of it. Look at us here – witwoo!

The bestest friends a
girl could ask for.

The first car in its
original glory... oops!
LOL.

Our first publicity stunt. My God we were cold!

Scramble, Egg and Toast. RIP.

Going in and coming out
of Celebrity Big Brother –
something I will never forget.

After my many Celebrity Juice appearances, me and Keith liked to get mortal!

Me and my second mam, Carol.

like him before —where we lived all the boys wore little vests and had orange tans and muscles – but Dan was from London. It felt like I had a foreign friend! Dan was a student and at one point during my living-in-the-car episode, I turned up at his student accommodation, knocking on the door.

'What the hell are you doing, Charlotte?' he laughed, looking down at this forlorn figure that looked like she hadn't washed for a week.

'I'm so lost, Dan. I've got nowhere to go. I've been having to stay in me car.'

So he let me sleep on the settee in his university house. The next morning he gave me a toothbrush and I remember as I stood cleaning my teeth he was looking at me, laughing his head off. I was giggling, too – I thought we were just having a mutual laugh at the situation I'd found myself in with the car – and we were cracking up for ages. Then after I'd finished cleaning my teeth he said, 'That toothbrush was out of the bin.'

Oh my God!

It's only looking back now that I realise how awful I was being to my poor parents. God, I feel bad for how I used to behave – the things I put me mam through! She must have been really worried. Eventually I did go home (I think I was running out of clean knickers). Mam was all over me, telling me she'd missed me and making me all my favourite food as a treat. I'd managed to turn what should have been a massive punishment into a huge welcome-home party!

I was always going missing from home, but usually for no

more than a couple of days at a time. What can I say? I was wild and crazy! I'd go out on a Friday, lose track of time and all of a sudden me mam would be on the phone and it would be Sunday and I'd be at a house party somewhere.

'What are you doing, Charlotte? You haven't been home for forty-eight hours!'

'I'm only YOUNG! Chill out, man!'

Melissa reminded me the other day about a time I phoned her asking if she and her boyfriend could pick me up from a bush by the side of the road! I'd been out all night and must've passed out; when I woke up I was lying sideways on a bike with one wheel and couldn't remember anything. I was still drunk. How the hell I got hold of a bike with one wheel I'll never know. But I was only young. Chill out, man!

My memories of fun times go hand in hand with my job in Tonic. Tonic is a small bar/restaurant right in the middle of Sunderland. It wasn't ever like work; it was like my second home. Mam got me a job there washing dishes in the kitchen when I was fifteen and I slowly worked my way up to kitchen assistant (I was allowed to flip burgers – woo hoo!), then when I turned eighteen I was let loose in the bar itself, taking orders, pulling the pints and serving people. The people who worked at Tonic were like my second family and I worked there for five years.

I can honestly say that working in Tonic for those five years were the best days of my life – even better than school. I had a job, I had responsibility and I felt like a grown up. I was always messing about and every day we'd have such a laugh – I used to streak topless down the back lane when I was putting the bins out and would slide down the back stairs in one of the big breadbaskets that the bread got dropped off in (they made great sledges).

Donna was the general manager and above her was a woman called Lorraine. Lorraine never used to speak to me; she didn't seem to know my name. I was just known as 'the girl in the kitchen'. She must have been really rich, because she and her husband owned all the popular bars in town. Whenever she came to Tonic, she'd pull up in this massive car, flicking her gorgeous long hair about. She was always tanned; she had a boob job and veneers. I was in awe of her but scared at the same time.

Donna was related to Lorraine but she was one down on the evolutionary food chain of bosses so was more involved with the staff. Donna always used to laugh at me but she could tell me off and I'd be frightened of her too. Then there was Becs, the supervisor, who was more like an older sister to me. The staff consisted of me, Kaleigh, Barbie, Norma and Lindsay – and I adored every single one of them. We spent most of our days pissing ourselves laughing (*literally* in my case).

I used to get away with murder working there. I'd regularly turn up to work an hour late, still in my dressing gown because I was hungover and couldn't be bothered to change. Becs would open the door, shake her head and laugh, 'Charlotte, this is getting out of control!'

The thing is, I knew they would never sack me. We had

a mutual love for each other, me and Tonic, and I couldn't stay away even if I wanted to. I'd work there in the day, and then when I had a night off I'd spend most evenings in there with my mates. I knew that because they were all like my family, if I got too mortal drunk, they'd get me home safely.

One night I drank so much that I fell asleep in the toilet (I can fall asleep anywhere at anytime). My friends were running around the bar desperately looking for me; they didn't have a clue where I was. Eventually they came into the toilet shouting my name and found me passed out, covered in poo. The good thing was, it wasn't my own poo (personally I think it's a bit better that I hadn't pooed myself, don't you?). The situation was this: you know when the toilet gets a bit messy on a night out? And there's sometimes poo up the sides and stuff? Well, the loo I'd chosen to have a sleep in had poo literally everywhere. All I can think is that I must've been trying to be sick, then I'd fallen asleep and my hand had slipped into the poo. These things happen.

My friends had to get the bouncers to carry me out – but the poor blokes were holding me really awkwardly, trying not to touch me too much in case the poo rubbed off on them. I stank. They put me in a taxi with instructions to take me home. About three minutes into the journey, however, the driver realised his passenger wasn't just pissed; she had poo all over her.

'Get out, I need to get this taxi cleaned!' he shouted.

'Whaaat?' I was still pretty jumbled and didn't know what was going on.

'And I need paying! I need damages!'

I had no money. My mates and I hardly *ever* had any money when we went out; we'd be lucky if we had a tenner each. We'd usually club together to buy a pitcher and the rest of the evening we'd 'minesweep', which meant we'd pick up the leftovers of other people's booze and mix it into one glass.

We'd get through our night out with no trouble, but it was always the taxi home we'd struggle with.

I tried to run away from the taxi driver, but he was too quick for my drunken floppy form and he grabbed me. Then . . . I kind of hit him.

'You've assaulted me! I'm calling the police!'

So that night I got locked up in a cell. The good thing about it was that they hosed me down beforehand so I was cleansed of poo before they put me in the special cellblock clothes. There was a female police officer who was really nice to me; she even brushed the poo and sick out of my hair.

In the morning me mam came to pick me up – I've never seen her so angry. The police officer said to her, 'She's a lovely girl, your daughter. And the plus side is, she's been tested for drugs and it came back negative.'

'Oh, I'm just *buzzing* about that,' Mam replied sarcastically.

Afterwards Mam had to track down the taxi driver because

he was going to press charges. She had to pay over fifty quid to get his car cleaned.

Places I've fallen asleep:

- On a speaker in a club – that was impressive because it was loud
- Numerous settees in clubs
- On the sitting room floor on NYE (I missed the whole of the NYE countdown)
- Toilet
- Stairs
- Floor
- In the bath
- My car

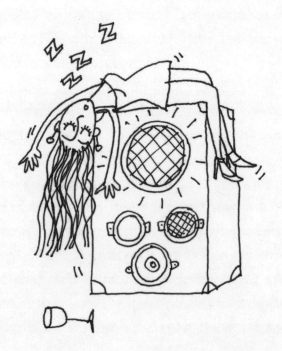

I could've happily worked in Tonic for the rest of my days, but Mam and Dad were desperate for me to get some kind of education. The problem was, I hadn't fathomed out what to do with my life. I was still hoping someone would just pay me and Natalie to make them funny videos but so far no one had come forward.

Seeing as Sixth Form hadn't worked out – what with 'Fightgate' and everything – I decided I'd try college instead. So I enrolled at a place called Bede Campus and opted for Law, Business and Psychology. I lasted for a few months. Once again I'd just made the wrong choices at the spur of the moment and then I found the subjects too hard.

After that I decided I wanted to study Criminology and me mam found out about a university course locally that would suit me so I enrolled. I'd decided I wanted to be a probation officer for young offenders. I'd been to a talk in Teesside by someone who'd been wrongly imprisoned and he had his probation officer with him – he kept saying how supportive the probation officer had been and I thought her job sounded amazing and really inspirational. I also loved children so I thought I could combine the two. To get into Sunderland University I needed to do an access course, and because I was a bit older this time, I found myself really wanting to do my best; I did all my homework and actually started to enjoy it. I was getting top marks for everything. I was buzzing! I was updating my Facebook status all the time: 'Another distinction!'

Then I saw an advert for *Geordie Shore* . . . and got totally, life-changingly, side-tracked.

9

SAVED BY *GEORDIE SHORE*

Some people would be mortified if their parents knew what they got up to on a night out and when people ask me about *Geordie Shore*, one of the first things they say to me is, 'Doesn't your mum mind what you get up to on the show?' But what they don't understand is that Letitia and Gary Crosby have seen me in *far* worse states than anything I've done on TV. Ask Letitia and Gary and they'd tell you that *Geordie Shore* calmed me down. Plus they knew that this time, when I was running round the streets being drunk and disorderly, I had a film crew keeping an eye on me and making sure I was safe.

I was on Facebook when I saw the advert.

Would you like to be part of a new TV show on MTV called Geordie Shore? *We want young single people . . . apply here.*

Whether I liked it or not, I was officially single. I'd split with Kevin and there was no sign of him taking me back (probably not helped by me climbing into bed with his dad). I was heartbroken. And I had nothing to lose.

All I had to do was answer a questionnaire.

What was your most embarrassing moment?

Easy. I wrote about the time I got covered in poo in the toilet in Tonic.

What would you say is the best part about you?

My legs and my bum. (For the record, I don't like my bum any more. Now I've lost weight it's gone dead flat. I'm going to focus on that this year.)

There were loads of other daft questions like: '*How many boyfriends have you had?*' and '*What's the craziest place you've had sex?*' (I obviously said it was when I'd had sex on a crate.)

I instinctively knew I needed to make the answers good but I had so many stupid stories anyway . . . this was easy!

The next thing I knew, I got a call.

'Hiya, we've got your form, Charlotte. We'd like to have a little half an hour phone interview with you if that's OK?'

I never expected that! I was shitting myself. I replied, 'Yes, can you call tomorrow at 3 p.m?'

I decided it would be better to talk to them at my friend Laura's house. I couldn't have me mam overhearing – she'd go nuts if she knew I was applying for some random TV show.

So the next day, I went to Laura's, got under her bedcovers and the phone started ringing. It was a woman called Lauren Benson who, unbeknownst to me, was soon to play a massive part in my life.

Lauren wanted to know more about my stories. We chatted for hours and had a real laugh and at the end of the call she said, 'Good to talk to you, Charlotte. I have a feeling we're going to be getting back to you for a face-to-face meeting.'

This was crazy. What the hell was happening? One thing's for sure, it was helping me forget about Kevin.

Besides, I'd had a premonition.

I think I'm a bit psychic; I have these visions. I don't get them very often but when I do – I DO! This particular time I was in the car and there was a song by Nicki Minaj and Drake playing on the radio. It's the one called 'Moment for Life' and as I was driving, I suddenly saw a vision of me on television – it was so clear. This song was the soundtrack, I was famous and I felt so great about everything, it was like it was happening for real. I was driving along feeling all gangsta in my Beetle and I was loving life, thinking, 'Who's Kevin now?!'

I've had three premonitions in my entire life. I had another one just before I went into *Celebrity Big Brother* – I got a vision that I was walking out of the door a winner (and that came true!). The latest one I had was about my clothing range Nostalgia doing really well (and it has!).

A few days after my phone call with Lauren, I was asked to come and meet the producers in person. Lauren was the casting producer and she introduced herself to me first. I felt an instant connection with her – she was small, with lovely blonde hair and the jolliest face you've ever seen. She reminded me of sunshine. I automatically felt so at ease with her.

The next people I met were two men – Eddie and Mike. Eddie looked exactly like the donkey from *Shrek* – small with big nostrils and curly hair – whereas Mike was a bit taller and he reminded me of an American even though he wasn't. They showed me into a room and I sat in front of a camera. They asked me all these questions, similar to the ones I was asked in the questionnaire. I answered them all but I made sure they sounded as rude as possible.

'What's the best part of a man?'

'His fingers because they're what do the stroking.'

They laughed. And as soon as they laughed I knew it was OK to carry on. All I ever want to do is make people laugh and it gave me such a buzz getting that reaction. Afterwards Lauren smiled and said, 'Great seeing you, Charlotte, we'll speak to you in a couple of days.'

I had a good feeling about this.

After that I was asked to go and meet the top people from London. This was a *big* thing – I'd never been to

London before (not that I was going now, they were coming to Newcastle to meet me). We met in one of the bars on the Quayside. I remember walking in and feeling really nervous. I'd done my hair in a massive bouffant and I had loads of foundation on and fake eyelashes. One of them was a man called Steve Regan and I could immediately tell he was important just by his aura – he made me feel intimidated and I knew I had to impress him. I soon loosened up. I regaled all my stories and everyone was laughing. That's when it all started to go wrong . . .

The others in *Geordie Shore* always brag about how the producers 'loved us straight away' but for me, it all went downhill from that meeting.

The next day I got a phone call.

'Hi, Charlotte, we've got a bit of a problem.'

My heart sank. I hadn't made it to the next stage, I was convinced of it.

'The people from London want to come up and see you one more time. They want to have another meeting with you.'

'Oh, why?' I was confused.

'Well, the thing is . . . they actually didn't believe any of the stories you told them.'

WHAT?

'Well, what am I meant to do?'

'Listen, Eddie, Mike and I think you're great and we obviously believe you but they just want to meet with you again one more time.'

My stories were so ridiculous that people didn't think they were real! Lauren continued to explain that she thought it was because I looked so sweet and innocent that in person I was the complete opposite to what they had expected. They found it hard to believe I was the same girl who did all these things.

Did they need proof? What the hell could I do to convince them? This was weird.

When Steve Regan came back to meet me, he sat me down and hit me with it straight away.

'The fact is, I don't believe anything you're saying.'

I was so taken aback with his bluntness. He was being really harsh and I was so nervous I started to cry.

'Now, Charlotte, don't get upset.'

'Well, I don't know what else to do!'

'We're just worried that if we put you in the house we're not going to see the real you at all.'

In the end I was with him for about forty minutes, trying to explain myself through the tears. I went home, certain I'd messed it up.

Then I got another phone call.

'We want you to come and do a psych test.'

Psych tests are things they make us take before and after every series to check everything's OK and that you haven't suddenly gone all mentally disturbed.

They asked me questions about my family life, then strange questions like, '*Have you ever been bullied?*' and '*How would you deal with negative comments?*'

94

I felt like I was really being analysed and it was almost like I'd done something wrong. I felt automatically guilty!

Next I was called back to a thing called 'green screen' – which was to become like second nature to me. Green screen is where we all sit and talk to camera about the events that have occurred in the show. It's called that because you're literally sat in front of a green screen – when the show is ready to air they use the screen to project an image from the show (usually the Tyne Bridge) behind us. What I didn't realise then was that what I was about to say to camera would end up being used in the trailer and the opening credits of the show. This is where I pipe up with the infamous cringey line about only dating men with six-packs.

I thought it was just another interview.

The producers fired all these questions at me about the sort of boys I liked and how I behaved when I was pissed. I sat there reeling off answers – I'd told them all of this before. How many times did I have to say it to convince them it was true?

'OK, Charlotte, we've just told you you're going into *Geordie Shore* – how do you react?'

'So you want me to act like I'm going in?'

'No, we've told you you're actually going in, Charlotte. You're in the show!'

'I don't understand. You want me to *pretend* to camera that I'm going in?'

'No, Charlotte, we're telling you you're in the house!'

'In real life? Or for the camera?'

They turned the cameras off.

'Charlotte. You're in the show, you start next week!'

'OH MY GOD! YEAAH!'

They quickly turned the camera back on to catch my reaction. I was punching the air. I walked out of that room and couldn't believe what had just happened.

In seven days' time my life would change for ever.

CHARLOTTE'S BUCKET LIST (THINGS TO DO BEFORE YOU DIE):

- Go whale watching
- Go on a safari
- Find an epic love/soulmate (done!)
- Grow my own fruit
- Fly through a rainbow in a helicopter
- Save a life
- Float in the Dead Sea
- See the pyramids
- Stand on grapes and make my own wine
- Go on a road trip around America

10

PARSNIP

Mam was not happy. I hadn't told her anything about *Geordie Shore* because I knew she'd freak out.

When I did finally tell her she just looked at me and said, 'You've had some stupid ideas, Charlotte, but this one just takes the pot.' I was starting to get my life back on track, I was about to get into university and all of a sudden I'd decided to go on a TV show for four weeks?

'Well, I'm doing what I want to do – I'm not listening to you!' I huffed.

'What about your course?'

97

'I'll catch up on everything I've missed, I'm only going to be gone for four weeks.'

I never did catch up on the work from my access course. (I also never forgot to remind Mam that if I'd taken her advice back then I wouldn't be where I am now. And I definitely wouldn't be sat here writing my own book!)

Geordie Shore was pitched as the UK's answer to the US show *Jersey Shore*. I'd never actually watched *Jersey Shore*. It wasn't until a few days before we went into the house that I decided I should have a look at an episode. I immediately regretted what I was about to do. One of the characters, Snooki, was pissed out of her skull in a Jacuzzi, kissing girls. Everyone else in the house *hated* her and I thought, 'What am I doing? I can't do this! It's so rude!'

In a nutshell, *Jersey Shore* is a reality show about a group of people from New Jersey who get put together in a house with a hot tub and get given loads of free booze so they'll all get off with each other. *Geordie Shore* is pretty much the same – except it's based in Newcastle which is colder and I think we have better taste in clothes than them.

Oh no! What was I going to pack?

Here's what I took with me to the *Geordie Shore* house:

- A pair of high-waisted silky pants with massive flared bottoms
- A black dress
- High heels – I wore them every night
- A couple of vest tops

To this day everyone still takes the piss that I only entered the house with about five pieces of clothing. The others all had massive great suitcases that could've filled Buckingham Palace.

Especially Vicky Pattison.

Vicky was already there when I arrived and I found her fascinating. She looked like a glamour girl – all massive hair, fake eyelashes and sparkles. I walked into the bedroom with my tiny little case, saw her Louis Vuitton luggage and designer heels sprawled across the bed and my jaw dropped. She was wearing a sparkly dress like she was on a night out and looked gorgeous. I was literally wearing a boob top that I'd pulled down into a dress, little cowboy boots and scruffy woollen socks. I didn't even have a bra on.

'Hiya, babe!' she said as soon as she saw me. 'Are your boobs real?'

She passed me a Jägerbomb, followed swiftly by a vodka Red Bull.

'Yeah.'

'Wow, they're so perky, babe!'

Vicky was one of those girls who call each other 'babe'. My mates and I never called each other 'babe'. Only the popular girls called each other 'babe'. Shit, I'm going to be friends with a popular girl.

I was so nervous and scared but Vicky was so friendly and I instantly loved her. We were boozing from the minute we got into that house and it wasn't long before I was so drunk I was following her around like a puppy, slurring, 'I'm so glad I met yoooou!'

The house itself was huge and was in a really expensive area where all the footballers used to live. It was over four storeys high and every bedroom had an en suite, there was a hot tub and an outhouse (which soon got the nickname 'the shag pad') and bowls brimming full of condoms in every corner (my first thought was, 'Wow they must have a lot of money to be able to buy all those condoms!'). The cameras were on us from the minute we set foot in the door – and they never stopped filming.

Sophie came in next and I knew straight away I'd get on with her. 'Oi oi, everybody!' she shouted and I felt a bit jealous of how outgoing she was. That night we got so drunk we were sent to bed early and when we woke up in the night we started bouncing all over the beds because of our excitement. I think I get a lot of my mannerisms and personality from Sophie – I applied them to myself because I wanted to be as fun as her. She's one of my best friends.

Then there was Holly. None of us were sure about her to start with. The Holly Hagan I met in the first series of *Geordie Shore* was a totally different person to the one I know now. She didn't know herself at all. She had a boyfriend called Dan but was always getting her boobs out and kissing other boys on camera! She was only young and was really immature. I reckon she properly came into herself in about the third series. She's had a big journey, that one.

Jay was a massive charva and was a ridiculous shade of orange. His eyebrows were far better than mine though.

Then there was James; he had a funny sideways fringe and gave me a guided tour of the house. I thought he was good-looking but I didn't fancy him. Then I got back downstairs and Gary came through the door . . .

He was tall, slim, with dark hair and a cheeky smile, and I could see through his top he had good muscles.

Oh God. I fancied him.

I didn't speak to him all that much the first night; I got way too drunk with Sophie. It wasn't until the second day when we were introduced to our boss Anna who told the boys they had to be naked butlers and they had to take their tops off . . . that's when I got a proper look at Gary in all his glory and thought, WOW.

No body fat.

Just muscles.

He *definitely* had a six-pack.

That night we all got dressed up to go out and I put on my skimpiest outfit. That's when the flirting began.

I remember us all being so enthusiastic about everything in that first series. We forgot the cameras were on us and for the next four weeks we had the most amazing time getting to know each other and developing a bond that would be unbreakable. The film crew had a little bedroom upstairs where they could get some kip overnight. But none of us ever wanted to go to bed – we were so excited!

We used to lie in bed talking for hours, getting to know

each other, chatting about our lives and the crazy things we'd got up to. We were all forming brand-new friendships. Gary and me would snuggle up in the double bed and chatter non-stop. Nowadays I struggle to get a sentence out of him! Gary's changed a lot throughout the show; the person I knew in series one is a different person to now.

I know it sounds stupid but when we were in that house we forgot about the outside world completely. We knew we were filming a TV programme but we didn't have a clue back then which bits would actually be shown on screen. We were acting like it was some sort of summer camp.

Even before the opening credits of the show there's a warning: *The following programme contains bad language and sexual references from the outset and throughout.*

That, to me, captures the whole spirit of *Geordie Shore*. It was just a load of young people having a laugh and not giving a shit about anything – because they didn't have to.

Sophie's intro to camera was dead funny. She said, 'I'm twenty-one, I'm going to be a complete slut and I'm going to put out. I like a big butch man with muscles and a golden tan but they cannot be as dark as me because that would be competition!'

James said, 'The hardest graft I've ever done is me hair,' which is something that has haunted him ever since.

And I really should've known to steer well clear of Gary from the moment he opened his mouth: 'I literally know pulling birds inside out, from the minute I get their number to the minute I shag them, I know that situation. I've got a pretty good secret weapon. It's literally the size of *that* . . .' (He then gets out a TV remote!)

There was also a guy in there called Greg but he only lasted one series and the Magaluf special. He was too boring. Vicky fancied him at first but then she ended up getting off with Jay – although they spent most of the time arguing. And that came to be normal where Vicky was concerned; I don't think she knew how *not* to have a row with someone. She was a head case! I still loved her, though. Vicky was used to being treated like a princess. She told me she always dated footballers and you could tell she was used to the VIP life – she was *very* confident.

While Vicky was rowing with Jay, Gary and I were embarking on what was to become the show's biggest never-quite-happened romance. On one of the first nights we were out in a club and he said to the lads, 'I'll take one for the team. I'm going to go home with Charlotte.' I don't know what he meant by that – maybe he wanted to be the first to get with me!

So he turned to me and said, 'If you want go back to the house, spoon, neck on, hot tub, whatever, then I'll pie everyone off and go home with you. I'm not shaggin' ya, though.' (This is a typical thing boys say to get a girl home when they mean exactly the opposite.)

'Why?' I asked, 'There's some mint girls in here.'

What I didn't know at the time was that he'd told the producers in green screen that he liked me. 'Her body is amazing,' he'd said. 'She's a pretty girl. Obviously not the prettiest but her banter is hilarious.'

We didn't have sex that first night but I did see his penis. He always boasted about how he had a big one and he was right.

I said to him, 'Keep that away from me!' I told the camera afterwards that he must've put a girl in hospital with that thing; he could have punctured her lung or something. The first time I saw it I thought, 'Oh my God, that is quite big!' I know it sounds weird but it reminded me of an adult man – stick with me on this one . . . imagine that instead of a willy you can see an *actual man* with a suit on, carrying a briefcase. That's what it looked like Gary had down there – this big man bobbing about! Obviously Gary made sure everyone else in the house saw it, too. Holly said it was like her forearm. 'It is huge,' she said. 'I would be scared!'

If I could turn back time I would not have spoken about his penis EVER. I certainly wouldn't have called it a parsnip given how much Gary LOVES that description. Because do you know what I get asked IN EVERY INTERVIEW? 'How's the parsnip?' That vegetable will haunt me for the rest of my life. All I get in the street is 'PARSNIP!' And when I'm doing nightclub PAs I get given parsnips! 'Charlotte, look what I've brought you!' I must've had about 700 of them by now. And I have to pretend no one has ever given them to me before so I don't hurt anyone's feelings.

I just want to spit on the things.

I hate parsnips.

When we finally did shag, I felt like he'd popped my brain out of my skull.

Gary was all over me one minute and then shagging another girl the next. I was beginning to like him and one day in green screen I told the cameras the thought of Gary with another girl made me think I might be sick in my mouth. Or poo myself. Or both.

Vicky said she thought me and Gary were destined to end up like a Shakespearean tragedy. Although at no point in Shakespeare's *Romeo and Juliet* do I remember Romeo referring to Juliet as his 'banker'.

That's what Gary started calling me – his 'banker'. This basically meant that he thought he 'had me in the bank' for any night he hadn't pulled. I was some cheque he could cash in at any time. Well, I'll tell you what, Gary Beadle – no one writes cheques any more!

I have to admit I did get a bit excited when Gary called me his girlfriend, though. Although that's not exactly what happened. What happened was, we all went go-karting and James was chatting to Gary and referred to me as his 'girlfriend' and Gary hadn't protested. Which is basically the same as him saying it himself.

Despite how Gary would be with other girls, these weird things would happen between us and sometimes I'd think, 'Maybe he does like me . . . Does that mean he cares *a little* bit?' But I was battling with my emotions because as the days went on, everyone started warning me off him. They'd constantly be telling me, 'He doesn't like you, Charlotte, he's doing it for the show.'

While I was on and off with Gary and Vicky was with Jay, Holly was feeling really left out. And one night she left the club we were in, came back to the house, packed her bags and left. The worst part was – we didn't even notice she'd gone.

I woke up in the morning to find a note she'd left me, saying I was the only person in the house who'd been there for her and that she loved me but had to leave. I got really upset. She might have been annoying but no one deserved to feel so ostracised that they have to leave.

You had to admire Holly, though; she had a thick skin. People had been pretty horrible behind her back because she'd been getting so drunk and behaving weirdly. She knew what everyone had been saying but returned after a few days and just carried on where she left off. Being annoying!

Gary's behaviour was getting worse, too: he was pulling girls and then expecting me to get into bed with him afterwards. The problem was, most of the time I was so mortal I just did it. But before long he was just making me feel rubbish again. I described it on camera as him pissing on the flame of my soft spot and said that the wind was blowing the ashes away. (I did come out with some weird shit in green screen.)

The problem was that Gary fancied Gary. Gary thought Gary was the best thing since sliced bread. Gary thought

Gary had the best vegetable in the grocery shop. And Gary thought Gary had the best body in the world.

Fair enough, he did have a six-pack but anyone can have a six-pack when they're the size of an actual stick. He hated anyone calling him skinny – it really wound him up. It was his Achilles heel and I'd always give Gary grief about his weight whenever I wanted to annoy him.

When I wasn't with Gary I spent most of the first series either falling asleep on the loo or singing stupid songs. I made one up over breakfast once about a sausage family sizzling away when one fell out of the pan and it was like the rogue son that had gone missing. I liked to make up little songs all the time but after I did the sausage song, everyone would nag me to do another one: 'Come on, Charlotte! Make up a song!' I wasn't a performing monkey! I could only do them when they came to my head!

Filming the show isn't like doing *Big Brother* where the cameras are all fixed and you don't know who's watching you. In the *Geordie Shore* house we got to hang out with the crew all the time, so they're almost like the housemates that don't appear on camera and you get so used to them being there that you forget what you're doing (I think *that* was obvious . . .).

You also had to get used to people talking about you behind your back, but without it I think the show wouldn't have been as exciting. In the first series we still didn't quite know what we wanted to say and at one point Vicky took it all the wrong way and kicked off because she said we'd been moaning about her to the boys. She started crying because she felt ignored. We were dead scared of Vicky at the time – she was such a dominant presence in the house that for her to think she'd been left out was weird. She was really angry. I think she would have continued to be that angry all the time if she hadn't eventually come to agree with me that this was what the show was about. She had to learn that you've got to talk about people! That's what makes it interesting.

We always felt like we were walking on eggshells with Vicky, right up until she left in series nine. It was like she was judging us all the time. Even though she could be amazing and lovely, you still never quite knew where you stood with her. I think I speak for everyone when I say there wasn't a moment when people didn't feel they had to tiptoe around her just so Volcano Vicky didn't erupt.

Meanwhile I kept trying and failing to stay away from the parsnip. Once I'd had a few drinks, that was it. It was sending brainwaves to my head. I was convinced at one point that Gary's willy really did have hypnotic powers.

Towards the end of that series I decided to tell Gary that I fancied him. We'd been sharing the same room in the house and I wanted to tell him that I liked him and I wouldn't be happy if he brought a girl back while I was asleep in the next bed. He assured me, 'I'd never do that: if I was going to bring anyone back I'd bring her into the shag pad.' Oh great.

So he was still saying he was going to pull . . . just that

he wouldn't do it next to me! That was hard to hear. It was also a big fat lie.

The next night Gary brought a girl back WHILE I WAS ASLEEP IN THE SAME ROOM. He obviously doesn't have the capacity to remember promises because he's so skinny they just drop out of his skinny little body!

I vowed I'd never ever eat a parsnip again and if I so much as set eyes on one I'd cut it into shreds and spit on it.

11

MORE MADNESS

The first series of *Geordie Shore* hadn't even aired yet when we got a phone call from MTV UK telling us the show was going to be broadcast in Australia. I'd never been to Australia in my life. Australia was on the other side of the world and I knew anything on the other side of the world was a big deal. Australia had always been talked about because it was UPSIDE DOWN. It took A DAY TO GET THERE. And I thought only rich people were allowed to go there.

'We're thinking about sending you and Gary to Australia for a week to do press and promotion . . .'

My jaw dropped.

'Whaaaaaat?'

They wanted ME to go to AUSTRALIA! Not only that but I was going with GARY.

Even though we'd had a big fall-out at the end of series one after he shagged a girl next to my head, a few weeks had passed and by now everything had been forgotten. We were all too excited to stay angry with anyone for long. Plus I really fancied him. And now I was going to be in an upside-down country with Gary, for a whole week, on our own!

When I told me mam she just said, 'What? Are you sure?!' No one could believe it. I phoned Gary and he was as excited as me. The fact that it had only been us two picked to go out of the whole cast made us think, 'Ooh, maybe they like us the best! We could be the favourites!' (Although as it turned out, after the first series aired, we weren't the most popular at all – everyone seemed to love Jay and Vicky the most.)

We got on the plane. It should have been the most exciting plane journey ever – we could have drunk loads of booze, watched films, had a snog; we could even have joined the mile-high club! But no, instead Gary slept the whole way.

When we landed and walked out of the airport in Sydney, we were picked up by this big black Mercedes and there were paps everywhere! It was like we were royalty or some-thing. Did they actually have a clue who the hell we were?

We were driven to an amazing plush hotel with our own suites and these fancy bathrooms and giant beds. I'd never seen anything like it – we were being treated like proper famous people.

We'd been invited to a big party that MTV were throwing and it was here that I truly realised for the first time that Gary didn't actually like me at all. We slept together the night before in the hotel and I was starting to develop massive feelings for him again, but as soon as we got to the party he barely acknowledged me.

It never seemed like he wanted to spend time with me at all.

Suddenly we were stood in this room expected to mingle with all these famous people like Audrina Patridge from *The Hills*. Everyone kept saying, 'Wait until she gets here!' They were talking about this famous sportswoman. Gary asked someone what she looked like and they showed us a picture. His tongue was hanging out of his mouth. 'Oh my God, she's unreal, she's so fit!'

I felt like shit.

Then she turned up. There was no denying she was hot. Her body was incredible and she had this blonde flowing hair and a tan to die for (a real tan, not a fake orange one like mine). As she shimmied across the room, all I could think was that I could never look like her and it made me feel really sad.

She and Gary were flirting from the minute she walked in.

He kept disappearing off with her, leaving me on my own with no one to talk to. He was the only one I knew there! He was my friend! I was just this girl who hadn't even been on telly yet and as I looked round the room I felt so intimidated. One girl, a presenter called Daisy, started talking to me. She was really nice and we had a laugh. Then after a few drinks she turned to me and said, 'You do know Gary's gone home with her, don't you?'

My heart was broken. It made zero difference to Gary that we'd slept together the night before. I got a taxi back to the hotel and when I woke up the next day the press were calling my phone. Not only that, but they were outside the hotel! All they wanted to know was one thing – 'Has Gary slept with her?'

Turns out this woman was in a relationship. Of course they both denied everything. But I didn't believe it. This was Gary, after all.

The next trip abroad was Magaluf. We were all sent there for a series special: *Geordie Shore – Magaluf Madness!* This was on another level to being in the *Geordie Shore* house. We had our own fancy villa with a pool! It didn't quite turn into the fun first night we might have liked, though. On the first night the girls had a huge fall-out with the boys because we snuck out when we were supposed to be looking after the house. We all ended up pulling and brought boys back with us, and the boys had a shit night! So for a couple of days it became this divide. The villa was like a war zone: boys v. girls. It got pretty nasty. The boys were really angry that we'd broken the rules and they started lashing out. They could be right bitches when they wanted to be! After everything we'd been through, Gary called me 'fat and ugly'. And it really hurt.

In the same way I knew he hated being called skinny, Gary knew he could hurt me by calling me names like that. He was preying on my insecurities and deliberately trying to make me feel like poo. Every time I argued with Gary I was either called ugly or a slag. It got to the stage that before I went down to the pool in the morning I'd find myself putting makeup on. I had always felt comfortable with who I was, happy in my own skin, but he was messing with my mind. I'd never cared what I looked like, then all of a sudden I was comparing myself to every girl that he'd pulled. It was a downward spiral of horribleness. For a boy to make me feel like that when I'd never felt like it before was awful. I just felt ugly all the time.

'Charlotte, do you want to spoon or not?'

Before long, Gary was worming his way back into my affections and somehow I was falling for it. He would ask me to spoon him in bed and then the next day he'd raise an eyebrow at what had inevitably just happened: 'Well, spooning does lead to forking!'

After I'd slept with him again, I bashed the pillow against the wall in anger. I hated Gary. I felt so bad about myself. I crept out and slept on the sofa. I didn't want to admit it to Sophie and Vicky. They soon guessed, though, when they found me in the bathroom crying. I couldn't handle these emotions. What was happening to me?

Obviously the next day, as soon as we were so much as breathing the same air as other human beings, Gary was off shagging someone else. I couldn't carry on like this. So when he was on his own I marched up to him and said, 'I'm out of your league . . . I'm not your banker any more. This is it.' After I'd done it I felt so powerful. I was like Rocky running up the stairs to victory!

He'd made me feel ugly before but now I was confident and in control once more.

What we didn't yet know was that public were starting to like the 'Gary and Charlotte' thing. After the show had aired on TV, we'd get messages saying 'you two are made for each other' and some people would even call it 'the Gary and Charlotte show'. So naturally, the others began to begrudge us for it. Greg (yep, the one who was about to leave because he's too boring) used to ring me up and say, 'Charlotte, you dare get with Gary next time! Don't do it, he does nothing but use you.' Vicky was also warning me off Gary: 'Don't go near him, he's using you. The more you go near him you're giving him what he wants. He thinks he's King Gary!'

I didn't know what to think. Gary and me were still close, so I would tell him what people had said and then he'd be furious. Because he was so angry I'd think, 'It can't be true.' But then I started thinking, 'Or he could be angry because it *is* true and he's been caught out.' I was confused.

Either way, tensions were mounting and we weren't even back in the house for series two yet . . .

* * *

The next series was definitely an explosive one. In episode one, Vicky was in an 'unshakeable relationship' with a guy called Dan and by the end of the series she was madly in love with our new housemate, Ricci Guarnaccio. There was also another new addition in the form of Rebecca Walker.

When I first saw Ricci I thought he was good-looking but because he wasn't very tall he reminded me of a Smurf.

Rebecca was pretty with long dark hair. When Becca came in it really shook the house up because she didn't give a shit about anything. Becca was only in the show for a couple of series but I'd love her to come back in again – she was so feisty, it was just what we needed.

This time round, Sophie had a boyfriend too – a guy called Joel from London – and Holly only wore one pair of eyelashes at a time (she used to wear about nine). It was all change! Well, apart from Gary and me. Mam warned me not to go near Gary this time; she and me dad *hated* him for how he was treating me. She said he was bad news so I had to promise that if I did anything with him I'd do all the ironing for a year. Even though I couldn't iron. She even told him to his face on camera at one point!

Sophie's boyfriend Joel was a talent organiser (or something like that) at MTV and when Sophie met him she used to go on about how much she fancied him. He started wanting to be involved in the show and for a while we thought he had ulterior motives and he was just using her because he wanted to be on TV. And it took us a good four series before we realised this wasn't true.

We weren't living in the same place as before for this series, we were in a totally different house. I say 'house' but you couldn't really call it that. This one – which is the same house we've been in ever since – was basically a shell that should be a factory in a business park on the bank of the Tyne. When you first entered, it looked incredible – because it was basically like a massive studio set, so the lounge and kitchen were all open plan and it looked huge and really fancy. It has two giant bedrooms for nine people and only one wardrobe in each bedroom, which is why we have suitcases all over the floor all the time. We couldn't stay in the proper house we had in the first series because we got so many complaints from the neighbours – they said we 'devalued' the whole of the street. We got a really bad name (although I thought it was really funny).

No matter what had gone on between us, me and Gary still had a special bond and were really close. I described it as being like 'the friendship of two small otters sharing a log'. But nevertheless I was determined to be an independent woman and not let him use me whenever he felt like it. As far as Gary was concerned, 'the bank' had been demolished and in its place was a women's shop. And if anyone was to come in asking for a cash point, the independent woman who worked there would smash his face in!

But the first night we were all back together, when Gary was on the pull again, I felt really jealous. I couldn't help myself.

Ricci was a gentleman and took me home that night to look after me but Gary barely noticed. The next morning all I heard was that Gary was in the shag pad with the girl. I was angry and upset that I'd allowed myself to feel so shit and was back to being in the same situation all over again.

I decided to have a chat with Gary and be honest with him. I told him I was insecure and that I wanted to spit in the eye of any girl who came near him. He just laughed.

We had a new job this series – our boss Anna had decided we were going to be spray tanners. Looking back over the series I don't think we realised quite how much tan we'd been putting on ourselves, let alone anyone else. We'd been caking it all over our bodies and didn't have a clue how bad it looked on camera. When I watch it back, we just looked dirty!

From series one to three we were a deep shade of mahogany.

From four to five we were a deep shade of orange.

Then after that we were a really light diarrhoea colour. Which in my mind is the perfect hue to ask for if you're ever getting a spray tan.

I was still in bits about Gary and spent my first day as a spray tanner just getting extremely pissed on the job. So drunk that when I got back to the house I decided it made perfect sense to hunt down the parsnip and . . . I slept with him again.

Night after night I'd watch as Gary pulled another girl in front of me. I'd go home crying my eyes out and then,

119

on the odd occasion he wasn't with a girl in the shag pad, I'd climb in with him myself. I was letting him use me over and over. And I couldn't help myself.

So one day I decided I'd had enough. My emotions were all over the place and I didn't feel like myself any more. I just wanted me mam. Sophie cried and said she didn't want to be in the house without me, but I knew I had to go. Everyone was in a state of shock – I think the poor girls felt guilty as if somehow they'd fucked up.

I only stayed away for a few days. Then Gary came knocking on the door of me mam and dad's, trying to persuade me to come back. He told me everyone needed me in the house because everyone missed me. Mam told Gary on camera that he wasn't allowed to shag me again which was really embarrassing. As we drove back to the house I felt confused. I told him, 'It's not that I've stopped caring, Gary, it's just that I now realise *you* never cared.' Then Gary said, 'I have missed you. Maybe we should give it some kind of a go as boyfriend and girlfriend?'

But I didn't want Gary as a boyfriend. I'd had time to think and I knew it wouldn't be right.

I still shagged him, though. This time we did it in the shower.

We also did it in Ricci's nan's bed. Me, Vicky and Gary went with Ricci to visit his family for the night. When his mam and dad asked if me and Gary were girlfriend and boyfriend, I replied, 'No, we're close friends who get naked in front of each other.'

We stayed in Ricci's nan's bed and we were laughing so much that I weed myself. It was the funniest moment ever. Miles the cameraman was in the bedroom with us. We're so close with the crew that sometimes I think they forget what they're there to do – they'll be sat in the room and we'll be like, 'Er, can you go now?' because we either want to go to bed or shag.

We got under the quilt, Gary got on top of me and I still had my top and knickers on and I farted. *Really loudly*. Because we were under the quilt Gary got a massive waft of it in his face and it stank. Miles was laughing so hard the camera was shaking. And that's when I laughed so much I did a wee in the bed. (I felt awful afterwards but Ricci told me not to worry and that it was actually a spare bed after all.)

Believe it or not, Vicky was still in her 'unshakeable relationship' with her boyfriend Dan at this time (although to be fair she had tried to end it with him on several occasions and he kept persuading her against it), but Ricci was laying on the charm big style. For her birthday he bought her a massive great giant teddy and loads of flowers and she was like putty in his hands. A few hours later, the doorbell rang and Dan had sent her a designer handbag and some Louboutins (which made Ricci's present look like it was for a five-year-old in comparison). Ricci was undeterred – he was cooking her candlelit meals and playing romantic music. In the end I was getting a bit sick of his horrible girlie soppiness, he might as well have had a vagina.

We threw a house party halfway through the series – this one was a 'silent disco' where you had to wear headphones with the music playing, and when you took them off to chat to people it was dead quiet. It was nuts! Gary had been pulling again since we got back from Ricci's family's house so at the party, I started getting it on with Ricci's mate, Leroy. It made me feel empowered – like the girl version of George Bush. Which I guess would have been Margaret Thatcher.

The cast gave Gary the nickname 'King Gary' because if he ever feels like he's in danger of looking like a bit of a mug it seems that somehow he'll manage to turn it around to his advantage. And the events that unfolded at the silent disco demonstrated this. When Gary saw me chatting and getting on with Ricci's mate Leroy, it seemed obvious to me that Gary didn't like it. It was as if by bringing his mate into the house, Ricci was threatening his territory. Sure, Gary didn't really want me, but he definitely didn't want anyone else to have me either. I don't think Gary would have wanted the cameras to see he was bothered, so instead he waited until Ricci went to the toilet – I reckon because he knew there were no cameras in there – and then he started having a go at him. Then when Ricci was walking out of the toilet, he was naturally carrying on the argument but Gary was now acting like nothing had happened, trying to make it look like it was all Ricci's doing! And because Ricci had a fiery temper when he was drunk anyway, it just looked like another run-of-the-mill Ricci kick-off. So Ricci started having a massive fight with Gary and it all went mental – James tried to split them up and the crew had to come into the set and pull them apart. Gary denies to this day that the fight was anything to do with Leroy and me but why else would he start with Ricci, Leroy's friend?!

Anna sent them both away as a punishment.

One time we really got to the lads was the night us girls decided to play a trick on them and sabotage the hot tub while they were out. We threw everything in it – gravy, chairs, chocolate sauce, fake tan, tomato sauce. This was another girl power moment – we decided we didn't want them to bring any girls back so we hid the mattress in the shag pad and ruined the hot tub so they couldn't go in there. It was sooo funny! But the boys didn't find it quite as hilarious as we did; in fact they went crazy when they came back – not helped by the fact that they all returned home alone as no one had pulled! As soon as they saw the mess it all kicked off. It was like they were the parents and we were naughty little kids and we had a massive row which resulted in James calling us all fat slags. Sophie was on the verge of knocking him out – she was really upset. You can't just throw names like that around. Once again there was a big girl/boy divide. Gary and Ricci had been let back in the house, but me and Gary definitely weren't 'otters sharing a log' any more – we were otters on very separate logs. And although Ricci and Vicky were an official couple by now and she'd dumped Dan, they actually split up over the hot tub situation (and this was just the start of one of many rows between the pair of them).

Holly really fancied James in this series and kept trying to do things to make him jealous – like having sex with someone else in a bed next to him and making really over-the-top orgasm noises (although all that did was put him off more!). You had to give it to her, though; she was very persistent and did eventually end up in bed with him by the end of the series.

As usual we ended the series with another big house party. Sophie's boyfriend Joel turned up – they'd been on and off all series so he really needed to prove himself to her. He rocked up in a vest that said 'male model' and started flirting with all the girls there. Then he said to the lads, 'You can't keep a player down,' which made us all hate him. He was being a real dickhead. We didn't want him in the house or near us and Sophie found it really difficult because she was head over heels in love with him. It was really hard for her at the time. We held this grudge against Joel for about three more series after that and that's when Sophie left the show. But they're still together so there was obviously something there! I've spent loads more time with him outside of the show and I really think he's proved himself now. He's actually really funny. Looking back, I think maybe he was just saying stupid things because he was showing off and trying to be one of the lads.

To seal the end of the series, Gary and me had sex – this time in the same room as Holly and James (she finally got her way). You just had to sniff the air in that room and you'd probably get pregnant. Gary told the cameras that he would 'probably marry Charlotte in ten years' time'. Once again he was determined to keep messing with my head . . .

12

WEEEEE... (AND POO)

Despite being in a television show I was still totally skint! I'd be borrowing £50 a month from my mum. Sophie would come to stay and we'd go out with £10 each to this club called Riverside (we'd get in for free because we filmed there) and we'd be able to afford one pitcher of vodka and Red Bull and then we'd minesweep like I used to with my mates from school. We'd only be able to afford to get a taxi halfway back to the house – we'd have to walk the rest of the way! But we were on such a high and loving life – we didn't have a care in the world.

All of the cast became really close mates and would see each other loads in between filming. I would invite the *Geordie Shore* lot to stay at my house and rather than just having to contend with one drunken daughter, me poor mam and dad would have to look after all of us. One night we went to an event in Newcastle and all lost each other so ended up coming back to my house one by one – with no money!

Dad says the first person arrived in a taxi at 2 a.m. and rang the doorbell.

'Hi, Gary, I've got no money . . .'

'Where's Charlotte?'

'I've lost her.'

Dad had to pay the taxi.

Half an hour later another one turned up and Dad had to pay for their cab, too.

I didn't arrive until about 5 a.m. and apparently fell through the door, went upstairs and slumped on the toilet. Dad followed me. 'Charlotte, your taxi's still outside! Have you paid?'

I batted him away like a fly.

By now me mam was out of bed, too. 'Have you got any money?' she demanded.

I rummaged in my handbag and handed her a pound coin.

Mam went ballistic.

Eventually Dad had to give the taxi driver a cheque because he'd run out of money. Mum was ranting: 'We went to bed at 2 a.m. and now we're over a hundred quid lighter, and we haven't even left the house!'

'Well, it's not my fault,' I shrugged.

'You've got two mates in the front room and they've all come home in the space of half an hour of each other – you were all in the same bloody venue but we had to pay for three separate taxis, and when I said, "Have you got any money?" you gave me a friggin' pound!' she screamed.

In the morning the gang were really sheepish. 'We'll drop the money off later – sorry Gary and Letitia.'

Dad was exasperated. 'If you'd actually stick together on a night out you'd save a fortune!'

We were starting to get recognised more and more on nights out. Half the reason the boys pulled so many girls on *Geordie Shore* is because they were targeted by fame-seekers. Whenever we're out in a club, the girls and me will have a good laugh and dance around but the boys just do this thing that we call 'meerkating'. They stand there half-talking to each other, and only then because they have to, while their heads are bolt upright, scanning the crowd for girls. That's all their nights have ever consisted of. They're not even having a laugh! Nowadays whenever we're out, there's a line of girls waiting for them, all pulling their best 'sexy faces'. These girls are so desperate to be picked – all they want is to come into the VIP area and be invited back to the shag pad. One night we were out and Scott (who joined in series four) had a flock of about ten girls around him and he was kissing all of them! We told him we had to go home so he had to pick someone to bring back with him. He couldn't decide so he got these ten girls to stand in a line and they were begging him to pick them! It was like an audition for *The X Factor*. I think he even ended up picking two in the end.

We did live the life, though. We got to go to Mexico in series three and it was amazing. We arrived at the villa and it was like we were in a mansion, it had its own pool and a giant staircase. We thought, 'Right, we've made it!'

Instead of Anna we had a boss called Cancun Chris – he was hilarious. He was so deadpan and so angry all the time I thought he must have been an actor. But he never broke out of character and we were always shit scared of him.

Cancun Chris told Becca we had to stay in and look after the house one night, but we rebelled and went out instead (obviously!) so we were sent away for three days to a grotty hotel in the middle of nowhere as punishment. The only good thing about being sent away was that Gary had plenty of time to miss me. As soon as I returned he admitted it wasn't the same without me there and as soon as he said that I felt like I was holding all the cards, which made a change. I was determined not to be all over him.

It was spring break when we were out there so there was plenty of opportunity for penis. I did pull but had too much to drink so instead of having sex I was sick in the sand.

For a while there, I felt like me and Gary had nailed the 'just being friends' thing. We even had a chat about it one night and I cried because I was so happy we were getting on so well. I told him, 'We'll be friends for ever,' and we hugged.

Vicky and Ricci were full on into their relationship by now (he even proposed to her at the end of this series!) and although they fought like cats and dogs, I could see how much he adored her. I knew I wanted someone who felt that way about me. I wanted to find someone who was right for me and I knew that Gary just wasn't that person.

Jay was in love, too – so in love in fact that he left at the end of this series to be with his girlfriend. We were in bits when he said his goodbyes, he'd been like the father figure in the house and we adored him. He was the first person we cared about who was taking the plunge and saying goodbye to the *Geordie Shore* life for good. I knew I was going to miss him so much, but I couldn't get my head around him wanting to leave. How could anyone be worth giving up all this for?

I had a few epiphanies in Mexico. I also had the shits quite a lot. One time I got them so badly I had to get rid of my pooey knickers – so I put them in a bag. And then I put them in the bin, in front of Gary. There was nothing I wouldn't show Gary – as me mam says, I have no boundaries. And it's because I do things like that that he could never go out with me. Gary likes his women to be ladies (or at least pretend they are). Whereas my boyfriend Mitch loves me for being me – I always poo in front of him. And sometimes we even sit on each other's laps while we're on the loo. I'd go so far as to say that pooing has brought us closer. Anyway, everyone poos. What's the big deal? Me mam pooed on my head when I was born.

I've got a bit of a reputation for pooing. There was one time at a *Geordie Shore* house party when I had really bad diarrhoea. The problem was that the *Geordie Shore* house only has two toilets – so whenever we have a few people round, there's always a queue for the loo.

This night, the toilet queue was too big for me to face. We were all upstairs chatting and Vicky was telling us an in-depth story and all I kept thinking was how much I needed the loo and that I couldn't go downstairs because the queue was so long. There was a mixing bowl in the room from when we were making a vagina mould in one of the episodes so Vicky told me to go in the bowl. I ended up emptying my entire bowels into that bowl (it was in front of Vicky but I think she just thought I was doing a wee)! There was diarrhoea poo and wee and the bowl was brimming and I put it back down in the corner of the room (sorry if you're reading this while eating your lunch – maybe this chapter should have come with a warning). We were so caught up in conversation that we forgot about my incident and headed back downstairs to the party. It wasn't until we came back up later to put our pyjamas on with a group of people and we were engrossed in conversation that suddenly someone said, 'What's that smell?'

One of the cameramen on duty that night was a guy called Mike and he'd been watching my every move (obviously – that was his job!). He told me afterwards that he was laughing at my reaction when people asked about the smell because he could see the recollection slowly dawn on me that it was my bowl of poo in the corner! So his camera followed me creeping over to where it was and he watched me slowly pick it up, hoping no one would notice. I went down the stairs clutching the bowl, weaving my way through the crowd as people started shouting, 'Charlotte, is that punch?'

'NO!'

I went into the bathroom and poured the whole thing down the sink . . . it went everywhere. Mike said he was retching just watching me. In the end the producers decided the footage was too disgusting to show on TV!

I also got a bit of my name for myself as a wee-a-lot. For some reason I've never been able to control my bladder and I'm always either wetting the bed or weeing in the sink (which I did once in the middle of the night in the *Geordie Shore* house . . . I still can't remember doing it. I think I was sleepwalking).

Here are some places I've done a wee:

- The toilet, that's a given
- A sink – once at nursery and also in the *Geordie Shore* house
- The bath – I do it all the time at home, and I even taught my brother Nathaniel to do it
- A bowl
- The hot tub
- The street

- The girls' bedroom bin in *Geordie Shore* – we all do that and sometimes it nearly overflows. Oh my God, the stench! We're so messy and unhygienic; we just don't care. By the end of each series, the whole house is a shithole. There was even a time when we weed *and* vomited in the bin and it was so full for ages that no one wanted to pick it up in case it leaked out of the side

- In bed – I did it all the time in *Geordie Shore* and once in *Celebrity Big Brother*. I usually get up and get a towel to lie on so I can still sleep. I also weed in Mitch's bed at his parents' house a couple of months ago. I was so mortified when I left the next day that I texted his mum, 'I'm so embarrassed about what happened last night, I've stripped the bed and I'm going to buy some more sheets, I'm so ashamed.' She texted me back: 'Don't worry, pissy knickers. What happens in Mitchell's bedroom stays in Mitchell's bedroom!'

13

'YOU'RE A DISGRACE!'

On the days we weren't being filmed getting pissed in the house or in a club (or rowing with one of our housemates!), we'd be called into green screen. We always have two down days a week set aside for this just so the producers can catch up on stuff. The cast gets to discuss what's been happening which gives the whole thing a bit of context and narrative. It's also our opportunity to vent about the others and slag them off if they've done something to upset us.

As well as the producers and researchers, there's a 'logger' who logs everything that's been filmed and when it comes to green screen, they have it all printed up. The producer reads through it with questions to prompt your memory like, 'Charlotte, Holly's telling you this . . . how do you feel about that?'

Sometimes if you've been in there for a good four-hour stint you have to have a break because your mouth ceases working and you stop making any sense. You've got to be in a good mood for green screen. You're fucked if your cat dies and you're meant to be talking about something funny!

The green screen studio is in the building opposite the *Geordie Shore* house and every time one of us goes over there and comes back to the house, the others demand to know how it has gone. 'What's happened? How did it go? Did it go well?' You want to know if the other person has been funny or not – because the most important thing (for me anyway!) is to make sure you've been the funniest. Someone might come back and sigh, 'It was shit, I literally didn't even get one laugh from the producers,' and you'd be thinking to yourself, 'YES!' We spend most of our time in green screen trying to outdo each other as much as possible – it's about saying the most awful thing we can think of just to get a laugh out of the producers. As the series has gone on, it's turned into a huge competition over who can say the rudest, most disgusting stuff.

The way we were behaving on TV was totally different to anything else out there and we were developing a pretty bad reputation in the media.

It got to me mam and dad more than it got to me. From the moment series one had aired there were reporters slating us and what the show was about. On the TV, in the papers . . . people would say we were a disgrace to Newcastle and that the way we behaved was a bad influence on young people.

Me mam got really angry at the way we were spoken about in the press and the backlash we got on the news. Her and me dad were really supportive of me and the show – she found the whole thing funny and could see it for what it was meant to be – a load of young people with no responsibilities just having a laugh and doing what most young people do. She got really wound up watching the news when reporters and politicians from Newcastle were saying, 'We're not having this show ruin our reputation!' They'd be on the telly talking about all the places of local interest that were apparently being overshadowed by our bad behaviour – 'what about the lovely places like the Sage [a venue for concerts and live music] and the BALTIC [a centre for contemporary art]? We don't want to lose tourism because of this tawdry show!'

Mam thought the whole thing stunk of hypocrisy. She'd shout at the TV: 'You lot need to get a grip here because the Sage is boring as hell and the BALTIC just has displays of coat-hangers in it!'

Mam was right, too. The truth was that most eighteen to thirty-five-year-olds knew Newcastle as how we were portraying it, as a fun party city. Mam would get really defensive about it because she said other young people going out and having a laugh on nights out in Newcastle weren't doing any less than we had done. The only difference was that our nights were televised. But the newsreaders carried on moaning and saying our show was disgusting.

Mam got so mad she actually rang into *The Wright Stuff* once. The TV presenter Matthew Wright was getting on his high horse about how disgraceful we were and Mam called him up. She got through to the researcher who said he was putting her onto the show but before Matthew got to speak to her she got scared and put the phone down.

It got to me dad, too. He was driving home from Scotland once and he was listening to a late-night radio show. They started talking about *Geordie Shore* and slating it. 'The parents must be so ashamed!' they were saying. Dad was fuming, shouting at the stereo: 'It couldn't be further from the truth!' He was about to pull the car over and ring in to the show but then a Newcastle taxi driver came on the air and did his job for him. 'You know what I think? You're all a bunch of hypocrites. They're just young people enjoying themselves. I see that type of behaviour every day, people coming into Newcastle and having fun. They're spending a fortune in the city and you should be proud of it!'

I used to tell my parents not to let it get to them. I don't know how but right from the start of the show, I've always been instilled with this feeling that any publicity is good publicity and that it's not worth listening to negativity. I've just never cared what people think. Everyone always says to me, 'You must feel so bad about it when people are slagging you off!' but I honestly don't give a toss. People always ask how I cope with all the nasty stuff that's said about me but I just think they're stupid to even ask me the question. I genuinely don't give a shit. I try not to care about what people who I've never even met say about me. I think there's always been a part of me that's thought that way. Even at school, whenever people said anything about me – whether it was me being a bad kisser (not any more!) or having a 'brace face' – I've learnt to try not to give a crap.

The bad publicity went on for a good two and a half years – it's only really now that people have started to realise *Geordie Shore* is a bit of fun and have taken it in the spirit it's meant.

CHARLOTTE'S WORDS OF WISDOM ON:
SOCIAL MEDIA

Social media can be a BITCH. It's full of trolls (I think that's what they call themselves) who, instead of sitting under the bridge waiting for the goats to cross, are sitting behind their computers sniggering at their really shit insults. (Because they sit at their computers all day I bet they have really bad posture.)

What I hate more than anything is other celebs pretending that they never get any bad comments on social media! WHO ARE THEY KIDDING? I get tons of bad stuff written about me. Some of it's pretty funny, but some of it can be quite hurtful. (And enough with the erections please, boys! I don't care how proud you are. Not for me thank you.)

At the end of the day, why does it even matter what these bunch of randoms are saying? As long as it's not coming from the people you love and are closest to, who actually gives a flying fuck?

My advice is to pause for a moment before you look at the computer screen and start reading through it all, fling your hands in the air like you just don't care and sing, *'I don't give a fuck, I don't give a fuck . . . oh no, I don't give a fuuuuuck!'* (Amazing song, totally appropriate for the situation. If you're not big on swearing, just replace the 'fuck' with 'damn'. It's not as gangsta, but it will do.)

Being on *Celebrity Big Brother* probably changed my fortunes the most but my mam is convinced that I'd always have come out of it 'reputation intact'. She says I remind her of Jade Goody because I'm not capable of pretending to be someone I'm not, I can't be anyone else other than me. And ultimately when someone's honest there's nothing not to like.

Mam and Dad never brag to their mates that their daughter is 'on telly' because they're not that sort of people. But whenever someone finds out who I am, Dad says they always say, 'Charlotte's our favourite!' and they get all chuffed and proud.

Most people would hate for their parents to see them

having sex, but that's one of many reasons me dad doesn't watch the show – he never even got to that point. When he first saw *Geordie Shore* he said it was the first time he'd seen me use the F word and switched off straightaway! He said it was like seeing someone completely different and that's why he couldn't watch it.

Mam loved the show, though – still does. I'd get the girls round and we'd have *Geordie Shore* parties when it was on. Dad would sit upstairs in bed with earplugs in!

Being on telly hasn't changed me that much. I guess it's made me grow up a bit – I've become a bit more independent and learnt about careers and money (I used to think I needed Euros go to London!). But I'm still just as stupid and have the same personality. Getting paid to be me has been pretty good so far!

14

FAME, FORTUNE AND FAIRYGATE

I was never very good at being 'a lady'. As well as having a bladder problem, I chew with my mouth open, I fart and I burp in public, I go out looking a mess in pyjamas and sometimes I walk around outside with no shoes on. But these are all things I choose to do because I don't mind what people think of me, and don't we all have the same bodily functions anyway? It's when that choice is taken away that things can become hurtful.

Ladies and gentlemen, allow me to present to you 'Fairygate': the time a full frontal of my fairy was shown to the whole country on national television – and I didn't have any control over it whatsoever . . .

It was during one of the earlier series of *Geordie Shore* and I was mortal drunk and climbing out of the hot tub. I was asking if someone would pass me a towel because I had no knickers on and I was worried my top would ride up. When you watched the episode on telly you can see EVERYTHING as I'm climbing out, and it's awful.

The night that episode aired on TV was one of the most horrible times of my life. I don't get sad about a lot of things, I'm normally strong and don't care what people have to say, but for the two days afterwards I sat in my house in Sunderland and was too embarrassed to go out. I thought everyone I met on the street would be talking about my vagina. I said to me mam, what if someone shouts, 'I've seen your fanny!' or if I heard people talking about me under their breath? I know this goes against what I've just said about people slagging you off but that's when it's about something you've said or a way you've behaved when you had control over what you were doing in the first place – not when it's about a part of your privates that you never asked to be put out there for the world to see.

Mam was horrified that it ended up onscreen.

It was all over Twitter – pictures of my exposed vagina were getting screen-shot and sent to me with the most shocking messages about how I was vile and disgusting.

Obviously the trolls sending these messages were far more vile and disgusting than the pictures of my fairy, but it still hurt. I couldn't go on Twitter for over a week. The producers apologised but 'sorry' didn't help. What is 'sorry' going to do for the fact that my vagina is now on Google images for ever and it looks awful? I was getting absolutely slated about it.

I felt very let down. I know we do a lot of stupid things on that show but we do it of our own free will. That night I was begging for a towel – 'Please will someone get us a towel?' – and when you watch it you can see I'm so drunk and I'm asking it so innocently. I'm still angry about it now but I never once thought about leaving because it was my job and I loved it most of the time. I was just dead angry and upset that my fairy was seen on telly – it looked like a shrivelled-up sugar puff on screen.

As you've probably realised by now, *Geordie Shore* isn't like many other places of work. You can't call in sick. It's not like other jobs because no one can stand in for me. I have to do my part. There have been times in *Geordie Shore* when my face has swollen so much from the flu I've I looked like Princess Fiona from *Shrek*. But you can get on with a lot of stuff when you you're enjoying yourself!

After series one, we were advised to get agents. This all felt really weird at first. Surely only Hollywood stars and people from *TOWIE* had agents? Sophie and I had a meeting set up for us with a big talent agency that had offices in London and up north. We met a woman who started telling us all this mind-blowing stuff: 'You can get endorsements

– clothing ranges, perfumes, books!' We looked at each other and thought, 'This is never going to happen to us!'

We signed with this woman, who was also looking after Jess Wright from *TOWIE* at the time. She was a good agent and at first I thought this was a great thing, but soon I found out that she lived, breathed and slept 'Jess Wright'! Even if she was with me and Sophie, all she'd talk about was Jess this and Jess that. One day we were sent to a photoshoot for *Nuts* magazine (that in itself was funny – I used to look at the girls in *Nuts* and think, 'They're so sexy, I could never do that!' And I'm still not very good at pulling sexy faces, no matter how much practice I've had. I always just feel really embarrassed). We were dead excited because we knew the photoshoot was a massive deal. But all our agent spoke about on the shoot was Jess! In the end it just made us feel crap, like she didn't care about us. So we decided to switch agents. We were introduced to Kate O'Shea from Bold Management and we're still with her now. She's brilliant. As soon as we met Kate we knew she was right for us; she was a bit older and really professional. After the first meeting with me and Sophie, we got worried that she wouldn't like us because we were so wild and she was dead organised and well put together. But it just worked and instantly we knew we could call her anytime about anything and she'd be so 'on it'. Without her in my life I don't think I'd have done half the things I've done. She's become like my second mam.

Being in the public eye has meant we've got to meet

some proper famous people, too. Sometimes I want to pinch myself when I think about the encounters I've had. I used to love Girls Aloud and Cheryl was always my favourite. I did like Sarah too because she was cool but I didn't really care about Nicola because she never said much. Then, a few years later I totally changed my mind about Nicola – because of her, I got to meet Cheryl!

I was with Sophie and my best friend Melissa and we'd got tickets to see Cheryl perform at Newcastle Arena. I was so desperate to meet Cheryl but didn't know how I was going to do it. Then I had a brainwave. I had quite a few followers on Twitter by now so I thought, 'I know, I'll tweet everyone to see if they can help me!' So I wrote: 'Everyone help! I want to meet Cheryl – please tweet her so we can go backstage!'

It was a bit desperate really but there you go.

To my luck, Nicola Roberts saw all the tweets and sent me a message, 'I've rung Cheryl and she knows you want to meet her.' She sorted it for us to go backstage! We were shaking and needed a wee. It was CHERYL COLE. We wobbled backstage to her dressing room, and when we got there she was with all her family (and a tiny little child who was weirdly also called Cheryl). She was really nice and started asking us how the show was doing. We got a few pictures and that was it – off we went. It was the most magical experience ever.

I saw her again recently when I was a guest on *Xtra Factor*. She was on the red carpet and turned and said, 'Hiya

Charlotte, you look amazing, don't you?' I was gobsmacked. Cheryl remembered ME. I couldn't believe it.

We were getting to mingle with proper famous people because all of a sudden we'd become famous ourselves! And one of the best moments I've EVER had was at the MTV Europe Music Awards in Germany. Me and the rest of the *Geordie Shore* cast were asked to present an award and because this meant going up on stage (i.e. doing something important), we got to be in the 'glam pit', which is where *all* the famous people sit. We had to get there during the day to rehearse and we were all standing backstage about to practise our lines when all of a sudden these big burly security guards started pushing us out of the way: 'Excuse me, make room! Make room!' Out of nowhere, in walked Kim Kardashian. She was right in front of us! So close that I wouldn't even have to put my arm out to touch her, I would literally have been able to extend a finger and I'd be stroking a Kardashian (I'd also probably have been arrested). She's so small and tiny up close and really skinny. AND breaking news: in real life her bum didn't even look big! My theory is that it only looks big because all those pap pics are taken with a wide-angled lens – the photographer is far away from her but their job is to make her look as close as possible and the wide-angled lens makes you look bigger than you actually are.

We were all stood with our mouths open, just staring, too scared to speak to her. She didn't even smile at us though, which I thought was quite rude.

That was our first celebrity encounter of the day, then

as we walked down from doing our rehearsal we saw The Hoff walking towards us. 'Oh my Gaaaad, are you the guys from *Geordie Shore?*' he drawled. 'Can I get a picture? My girlfriend loves you, she's from Wales.' The Hoff had asked for a picture and we'd just breathed the same air as Kim Kardashian – we were buzzing. We walked away from the stage feeling like all our Christmases had come at once.

Backstage there was a massive holding area where everyone's dressing rooms were located and we spent a good hour walking up and down the corridor looking at all the signs. We saw one saying 'Psy' (and started chanting 'Gangnam Style' at the door) and another saying 'Kanye West' – literally rows and rows of massively famous names. We were advised not to get our phones out and take pictures because we'd look like fans and it wasn't 'that kind of place'; because everyone was famous there you couldn't act like you weren't. But we didn't feel famous ourselves; we'd done about four series of *Geordie Shore* and we were totally in awe of what was going on and wanted to run around like school kids!

That evening we saw Psy waiting to go on and perform and then Taylor Swift walked past us to go in and she was beautiful – so tall and skinny, like a Hollywood movie star. She had red lips and was very pale (no orange faces like the rest of us) and her arms were long, her legs were long . . . she was just very LONG.

After we'd given out an award we got to sit in the glam pit to watch the show and Kim and Kanye were only a few seats in front of us. It must've been right at the start of them dating because I'm sure she was still with Kris Humphries in the show on E! Kanye was just very cool; you didn't see him laughing AT ALL. He was a bit taller than Kim but he was still really small. I'd like to have seen them stood next to Taylor Swift – they'd probably come up to her armpits.

15

SNIPPING THE PARSNIP

By series four I'd dyed my hair completely blonde. The sad part is that I did it because I knew Gary preferred blondes. I was dating a guy in the first few episodes but it was a weird relationship and I never really liked him. I don't know why I ever wanted to call him my boyfriend. I never even fancied him. I don't want to talk about him any more than that because he's not worth the space in this book.

We'd said goodbye to Becca and Jay at the end of the last series and now we were welcoming two new people into the house, Scotty T and Dan. Dan was always trying to fit in – he'd pretend he was so cool when clearly he wasn't and all the others would rip the piss out of him. He calmed down after a while though and everyone realised he was quite harmless. Scotty, on the other hand, didn't care about anything and was really funny. Dan only lasted one show but Scotty's still in *Geordie Shore* now. He's a handful and a nightmare but I love him. He was also a good match for Gary but unfortunately for me they got into a serious competition about who could pull the most birds.

Throughout series four and five my head was getting really messed up by Gary. This was when my feelings for him reached their peak and I spent a lot of time, both on and off camera, in floods of tears. He would pull loads of girls and still come back to me so I could never completely break away. At the end of series four we had a really intense goodbye where he picked me up and kissed me for ages and for some reason we were both really upset afterwards. It was very emotional. He was saying really nice stuff about me to camera, like how I 'lift a room' and other soppy shit. No wonder my head was in bits.

There'd been a point when we were so close that in between series Gary would come back to my house and stay. One night out he was so drunk he said, 'Charlotte, can I go back to yours?' so I gave him the key and he went back to my bed and I stayed out all night! In the morning me mam said to him, 'Oh hi, Gary, what are you doing here?' and he answered, 'Charlotte was meant to come back!' Mam made him breakfast in bed and he texted me saying, 'Charlotte, I'm at yours, where the hell are you?' That must have been the tightest we'd ever been. I can't imagine him coming back to mine now!

I really felt like I was stupidly in love with Gary. It wasn't the same as the love I have now for Mitch because that's 'returned love'. I love Mitch from the bottom of my heart and he loves me – we have a deep connection. But with Gary it was a one-way street. I had such strong feelings for this boy but I knew they were never going to be reciprocated; I knew he would never love me in the way I wanted him to. Every time I saw him with other girls my heart broke and I was convinced I'd never be able to get over him. That's when 'Psycho Charlotte' made an appearance. It was my coping mechanism, an outlet for all my emotions!

It was during series five that I truly started to get really down. We were doing 'Geordie Tours', which meant travelling to different cities in Europe to entertain stag and hen parties. During each flight, when the cameras were off, I'd sit with our series producer Amelia Brown and I'd be in tears because I was hurting so much. I didn't know what I was going to do any more. Amelia was lovely about it, she could see how bad I was feeling and she was really supportive and caring. But what could she really do? I was in love with someone I couldn't escape and I knew he'd never love me back.

The thing was, he'd sometimes give me a glimmer of hope that he did have feelings. Like when I first arrived in the house in series five – he put his hand to his heart and made a fluttering motion. What was that meant to mean?

We were sent to all these places like Amsterdam, Prague and Barcelona. Amsterdam was the coldest place I've ever been in my life (and I've been to the Arctic!). We had three nights there, and they were full on. We stayed in a house-boat and even though I was sharing a bed with Holly, I had sex with Gary IN THE SAME BED. She went mad: 'Charlotte, that's it now! You've gone too far!' She got her own back by telling everyone I was doing an American accent when I was having sex with Gary, but I don't think I was. I can't do a very good American accent for starters.

For some reason, one night I decided to go out in a pair of paper knickers that I'd made myself and stuck to my pubes with Sellotape. Sadly my 'disco clunge' ruined it (that's the name for when you get all sweaty down there). Luckily Holly had a spare pair of knickers – I told the camera this was because she had thrush and needed a change of pants in case she pulled! Holly and me went through a stage of telling lies about each other on camera for a laugh. I'd come out of green screen and tell her, 'I said a brilliant one about you, Holly!'

She'd be panicking: 'What? What?'

'You're going to hate it!' I'd laugh.

'Well, I'm going to make up a worse one about you!'

When we got back to Newcastle, Gary was back on the pull. So I decided to try speed dating. It wouldn't have been a bad idea apart from the fact that the first person who came and chatted to me was a boy who was suicidal. I said to him, 'Tell me something about yourself,' and he replied, 'I hate myself.' What was I supposed to say to that?!

Here are my tips for men when it comes to dating:

- Do be charming and confident
- Don't tell the girl she reminds you of an animal
- Don't show them your penis (Gary did that on his dates; he showed girls pictures of his penis)
- Don't ask about their favourite sex position
- Do be funny and witty
- Don't say you need a poo
- Do look nice
- Don't be suicidal
- Do have some self-esteem

After that I went on a date with someone called Graham.

We actually went on two dates and they were both awful. Holly came with me to the first one and for some reason I decided it would be a good idea to show him how I could do a fanny fart on the floor (well, I was just running out of things to do and there was no conversation!). The next date was ice-skating and it was the most awkward situation in my life. I was talking absolute shit and asking him if he would have sex with a prostitute.

I just kept thinking, 'Why aren't I with Gary?'

Besides, Gary had already found a way to ensure I was thinking about him on the date. He'd given me a special bell as a present and said it was for me to ring when I wanted him to rescue me from any situation I might be in. I looked at it: it had a leather heart on it. 'It's a love bell!' I thought. 'Gary has presented me with a love bell end!' He was trying to manipulate me and play me like a game of cards. But I'm not a game of cards. I'm a game of KerPlunk.

We were sent to Prague on another Geordie Tour. But unlike Amsterdam, Prague was amazing. Do you know how much we all loved the architecture in Prague? We were obsessed with it!

Absinthe was a big drink in Prague. One time we were going round the souvenir shops and Scotty T said to me, 'Come on, I'm bored of this, let's go and get absinthe and get mortal!'

So I jumped on his back and we went off in search of the green fairy – and it was the funniest day of my life. People told me afterwards it was their favourite scene of the series – we found this random shop with big hats, he bought a goat hat and I bought a deer hat and we went round Prague drinking absinthe and acting like idiots. The problem was, Gary didn't like it.

It was obvious that Gary could see that Scotty and me were developing a real bond and it seemed to me that Gary was determined to put a stop to it. Scott and me were being put together for a lot of things – working and going out – because we had good onscreen chemistry and were dead funny to watch. Scott's stupid and I'm stupid and together we're just idiots.

After our absinthe trip, we returned to the house and discovered that everyone had been asking where the hell we'd been. I could see Gary wasn't happy. He didn't like the fact that Scott and I had been getting along – that I had been spending time with a boy who wasn't him. It looked to me that Gary's way of trying to control the situation was to walk away whenever people were discussing what me and Scott had been up to. It felt like he was trying to avoid saying anything about us in case it came across like he was bothered in any way. But in reality, I think, he was fuming about the fact that Scott and I had spent any time together.

That night, when it was time to go to work on the stag and hen tours, Scott and me went alone which I could tell was winding Gary up. He was sooo desperate not to look like a mug! All I kept thinking was, 'I MADE GARY JEALOUS!'

After he made such a hoo-ha about me and Scott, Gary got drunker than he's ever been in his life and when we got back to the apartment he was throwing up – he was being violently sick and he'd never been like that before.

I put him to bed and we were both lying under the covers together and it was the one night he said 'something'. He said, 'Charlotte, I don't know what I'd do without you . . .'

I was silent.

'Charlotte?'

'Yeah?'

'I love you, you know.'

'You don't love us, you're drunk.'

'No, I really do.'

My heart was pounding. It had been all I'd wanted to hear for so long, but in my head I was thinking, 'He doesn't really, he's just saying it. He's mortal.' I'd been so conditioned to think he didn't care about me that even when he said it to my face I didn't believe it.

I remembered it the next morning but I didn't bring it up. His reaction?

He just said, 'Oh God, I was so drunk last night. God, I can't even remember anything I did!'

Classic excuse.

But once that episode aired on telly, everyone started going nuts about it: 'Oh my God, Gary said he loved Charlotte!' It was the first time he'd ever said anything like that and I was being sent hundreds of screen grabs of it – sometimes I still am!

It's when we got back to Newcastle after Prague that my feelings for Gary really started to hit me hard. He was acting like nothing had happened and pulling again. I was crying all the time.

Thank God I had my fish to come home and talk to. In series four I bought some pet fish – Scramble and Egg.

I used to tell them everything, they were the best listeners.

Egg was the most beautiful goldfish you've ever seen – he was round and fat and had a little belly and the prettiest tail, a bit like a mermaid. It was Egg's tail that I loved most about him. Egg was my favourite one – although I never

actually told him that because I didn't want to hurt Scramble's feelings. Egg was the cool fish, the popular one – the one who was funny and charming. Then there was Scramble who was a little bit ugly – you know how you always have an ugly friend? Well, that was him. He was clumsy and funny but a bit fat and spotty.

Scramble and Egg saw everything that went on in the house. They saw people going to the shag pad, they knew who started which fights, they saw girls doing the walk of shame in the mornings and booking taxis. They must have been mortified by it all. I think that's why Egg died in the end. Well, it wasn't actually that . . . it was because Scramble attacked him. He lived for a good two years, though.

Gary knew how much I loved them and when we used to argue he'd try and stab the tank with a fork to upset me! I know he did it because there was a dent on the glass once.

After another night of having to watch Gary on the pull, I'd had enough. I had a huge row with him back at the house – I chucked a spoon at him and he threw ham at me. It was the angriest I'd ever been. I smashed a lamp; I was screaming at him. Psycho Charlotte was out! The crew had to come and split us up in case we really hurt each other.

When I watched that episode back all I kept thinking was not 'How embarrassing!' but 'Wow, I really like my outfit . . . I've put it together really well!' I had purple lips and a bowler hat, and I kept thinking, 'That looks amazing!'

As for the lamp I flung? I break it every series, it's a curse. Everything you break you have to pay for, so it's typical that the thing I choose to break is a nice lamp while all Gary threw was a cheap piece of ham. They should have made him pay for the pig.

Our boss Anna told me I had to leave for a few days due to my bad behaviour. She said it was 'completely unaccept-able'. I think she just fancied Gary.

I wasn't the only one going all nutty over love. The Vicky and Ricci show was coming to a dramatic climax too.

Ricci's possessiveness was getting to the point where Vicky wasn't even allowed to get changed in the girls' bedroom, or wear clothes a certain length. She was becoming a shadow of who she was and we all knew it couldn't continue. As much as Vicky could be a bit nasty sometimes, we all loved her and being with Ricci was compromising the person she was. She wasn't Vicky any more and it was horrible to see. She left the house to get some space. And it wasn't long before the relationship was all over for good.

Once I was allowed back onto the show, the next trip was to Barcelona. I'd had plenty of time to think while I was away from Gary and I said to myself, 'I have to tell him how I feel, I can't keep this in any longer.'

I genuinely thought I loved him. But I know now it was just more of an obsession. I just *thought* that was how I felt.

I called the producer Amelia and said, 'I'm going to tell Gary something tonight.'

'What do you mean?'

'I'm going to tell Gary I love him and that I always have.'

'Whaaat? Are you sure you want to do that?' I could tell she was concerned.

'I don't know how else we're going to get this solved,' I told her. 'We can't just keep going backwards and forwards.'

Some producers might have thought, 'This is TV gold!' but Amelia was more worried about me than how it would look on TV. 'Just tell us if you change your mind; this is all your idea so it's completely up to you. If you feel you want to do it then just give us the nod and we'll find a place for you where you can sit and chat, just you and him.'

I hadn't wanted to do it in some noisy nightclub, you see, which is why I told the producer.

I told the girls, too. Holly and Sophie said, 'Shit, Charlotte, what the hell?!'

I think they knew he wasn't going to say it back. Whereas I was convinced he *would* . . . out of sympathy if nothing else.

We were on a little strip along the beach in Barcelona, sitting down having a few drinks. After a few minutes I gave the producers the nod that I was ready. We walked over to the little beach area by the steps. Suddenly I was very scared. This was getting very real. How the hell was I going to say this?

He didn't have a clue what was about to happen. We often had 'Gary and Charlotte time' on camera so none of this seemed odd to him. He didn't know what was coming.

I remember so clearly saying the words to him.

'Gary, I'm in love with you, I always have been.'

Then I saw his face.

The expression said it all. It was like I'd stabbed him and he was in pain. What I'd said was so painful to hear because he knew how hard it was for me to say it. And he knew how much it was going to hurt me to hear what he had to say back.

It was the words no girl wants said back to her.

'I love you to bits but . . .'

'I love you to bits?!' I love you to bits isn't the same as 'I love you' or 'I'm in love with you'. 'I love you to bits' means 'you're my best friend and I don't fancy you at all'.

'Char, I love you to bits, you know I do, but . . .'

I just burst into tears.

He hugged me. I was in shock.

This was awful! Why had I decided to do this? I don't know what possessed me! Why didn't anyone stop me? I felt like there was a weight off my shoulders but it didn't make me feel any better.

I didn't speak for the next few days. I was like the mute of Barcelona.

I cried the whole journey home. I could see Amelia felt so sorry for me. It had all gone so wrong.

I bought another fish to cheer myself up. Scramble and Egg now had a new mate – Toast. Toast was darker than the others; it was like he had a tan. He was tiny and had big googly eyes. He was completely different to the other fish and I was worried he wasn't going to fit in but he did.

We decided to have another house party to mark the end of that series and I should've known that it was going to kick off, but this was epic even by our standards.

It was fancy dress and the theme was 'American'. The girls had a chat first and decided we'd all go as something funny not sexy. I was sooo up for that – I love doing 'funny'. So I chose to go as Gene Simmons from Kiss. I painted my whole face white; I had the black makeup and stars all over my cheeks. Then I walked into the bedroom and Vicky was Batwoman – cleavage out, looking all sexy; Holly was a pirate – I'd never seen a sexier pirate in my life; and Sophie was a naughty schoolgirl! So I was standing there looking like I was wearing a black bin liner with massive baggy sleeves, a headband on, black lips, a guitar and the palest white face you've ever seen. It was a joke. To make things worse, people kept saying, 'Who are you again?'

Oh my GOD! I'm Gene Simmons!

Loads of other girls started arriving and they all looked so sexy – there were slutty cowgirls, girls in hotpants, bikinis, people dressed as Miss America. I felt like shit because Gary wouldn't look at me twice in this outfit. I knew who Gary was going to be looking at tonight and it wasn't going to be me.

The girl he ended up going with knew what was going on with me and Gary and I thought, 'How dare she have the cheek to come to our house party and rub it in my face?'

When Gary took her upstairs, I was standing on the kitchen bench. I don't know what came over me but I just jumped off – it was like I had superpowers. I felt myself flying in the air after them. I'd just told him I was in love with him and he takes a girl upstairs! Everyone was pushing and shoving, trying to pull me away. Vicky said it looked like a sale at Primark. Gary said afterwards he'd never seen such venom in my eyes. I was so upset.

Slowly but surely he'd broken me down. It had taken me so much courage to tell him how I felt. And now he'd destroyed me.

CHARLOTTE'S WORDS OF WISDOM ON: BOYS

Where do I even start?!

JUST DONT GO NEAR THEM.

OK, we all know that's impossible.

I hate to say this, but when it comes down to boys, your mam is always right. We like to think our mams don't know best and that we are perfectly capable of making our own decisions but, believe me, it's best to listen to the wise woman. Here's a message to me mam, Letitia:

'Mam, you are right and you always have been! I should have known when I developed my body parts in your womb and you kept me alive through that umbilical cord that you would be the one person who would know what's best for me. Instead I came sliding out of your vagina like Billy Big Balls, refusing breast milk, giving it the big one and I have been getting into trouble ever since. If only I had listened to you when I met my first boyfriend, Dan, who was way too old for me and a bit of a thug. When you said he was no good – YOU WERE RIGHT. Or if I had just listened to you with Kevin who finished me because he didn't love me any more – if I had just got on with my life like you said, then maybe I wouldn't have stalked him for four months, broken into his house and got into bed with his dad. YOU WERE RIGHT. And if only I'd NOT SLEPT WITH GARY! Is it too late to start listening now?'

16

MEETING MITCH: I'M IN LOVE

Being on TV means we get asked to do a lot of PAs (personal appearances) around the country – which basically consists of standing on stage with a microphone, trying to entertain a load of extremely pissed people. The first one I did was a disaster. It was just after series one and me and Greg (yep, the boring one) had been asked to go to a club in Cambridge. I knew it was going to be weird because Cambridge University was dead posh and had absolutely zilch in common with *Geordie Shore*. We arrived, were shoved onto the stage and stood there, rigid, like a pair of frightened rabbits. There were spotlights on us and I had the microphone in my hand. I looked out at the crowd and immediately froze. What the hell was I meant to say? No one had given us a briefing; we'd never done this before. All we'd been told was that we would be asked a few questions and now I was standing there like a lemon. Greg was hovering behind me on the stage, like he was about to run off at any second. My eyes focused on this boy standing towards the back of the club, who was staring at me menacingly. Before I knew it he put his hand up and started chanting, 'WHO ARE YA? WHO ARE YA?'

All of a sudden the whole club had started joining in. They were chanting it over and over again. From the corner of my eye, I could just about make out the shadow of Greg, shimmying backwards against the wall. He was trying to sneak off! I remained rooted to the spot, standing in the middle of the stage, frozen. I didn't know what to do.

Then, without so much as a hint of warning to my brain, out of my mouth came the following feeble words: 'I'm just a girl! I'm just a girl . . .'

I'd never heard my voice through a microphone before and it was echoing around the room. 'I'm just a girl!' was booming through the club sound system while everyone was still chanting, 'Who are ya? Who are ya?'

On the train on the way home I just kept shaking my head and repeating my words: 'I'm just a girl!' Why did I say that? What the hell? I think I must have intended to say, 'Please stop it, I'm just a girl . . .' but it came out a bit wrong. It was like my very own 'I carried a water-melon' moment.

When the others came back from doing their PAs they kept boasting about how great they were and how they got loads of cheers. But the reality was that no one would ever admit it if they got booed. I was the only one who was honest about it. I'd come back from mine and say, 'I got booed five times,' or 'I got a lime chucked at my head!' What was the point in lying?

We'd get about £100 to do an appearance and we were so chuffed – 'Wow!' we'd say, 'A hundred pounds!' The PAs were pretty bad at first; we had plastic glasses thrown and allsorts. I think it's because no one really cared who we were. Luckily that changed after a few series. And if it wasn't for a PA in Reading, I might never have met my boyfriend, Mitch.

I met Mitch through Gary's friend, Billy. Gary did a season in Malia one summer and that's where they became mates. Billy lived in London and we all got to know him pretty well over the series, so whenever we went to London to do press events or PAs we'd try and meet up with Billy for a night out.

One day I had a PA down south so I rang him up.

'Billy, I've got a PA in Reading. I've been given another hotel room so you can bring a friend. I'm bringing one of mine. Let's have a night out because we haven't seen each other in ages.'

'Charlotte, that sounds like an amazing idea!'

Meanwhile, in the background to all this, Instagram was starting to get really big and I'd been following Billy and noticed he had one particular friend who was always in his pictures. This friend had a bit of a beard and a lovely face, sort of like David Beckham, and I really fancied him. So like some kind of creepy stalker, I used to 'like' all of his photos. What I didn't realise was that I'd been doing it *quite* so obviously.

A few weeks later it was time for the PA. I didn't have a clue who Billy was bringing and it hadn't even crossed my mind it might be this friend because I don't like things like that. Set-ups make me feel really awkward; I hate any situation where I have to flirt. I'm not very good at it – I'm always convinced the guy won't like me.

I was in the hotel and I called Billy.

'Are you on your way?'

'Yes, can't wait to see you!'

'Who are you bringing then, Billy?'

I was lying on my bed, no makeup on, just chilling with my friend Melissa. I wanted to leave it to the last minute to get ready because I couldn't be bothered.

'Actually, it's funny you say that,' said Billy, 'because the friend I'm bringing is the one whose pictures you keep liking on Instagram.'

WHAT?!

'Who is it?' I said, trying to act cool.

'His name's Mitch.'

'Oh OK, that's great, I'll see you soon then . . .'

I put the phone down. Jumped out of bed. Ran into the bathroom and started plastering on my makeup and frantically doing my hair. He couldn't get here with me looking like this!

I REALLY FANCIED HIM.

You didn't get boys like that in Newcastle. He was a type of boy I'd never encountered before. He was like a man. He was like a manly man – he didn't have plucked eyebrows like the boys back home; he wore suits and was totally different from anyone I'd previously met. I thought he was *so handsome*.

I opened the door and it was love at first sight. I still remember what he was wearing – he was dressed in a thick brown cardi with a cream top underneath. He had on some jogging bottoms and there was a big brown bag slung over his shoulder. He dressed so nicely! He looked like a man who'd just stepped out of a Next catalogue. He was so tanned.

My heart was in my mouth.

The only issue was his height. I'm five foot six inches and he's about the same as me (except when I wear heels I'm a bit taller than him). But all of that soon fell by the wayside because I loved him instantly.

He was so cool. He walked into the room and spoke in this strange London accent, 'You all right, love? How ya doin'?'

He oozed so much confidence. He came in, gave me a kiss on the cheek, went over to Melissa and gave her a massive hug. Melissa is very weird with boys. She doesn't usually like being around them because she thinks they're cocky and they'll take the piss out of her. But he was *so* lovely to her.

We had adjoining rooms and we left the doors open while we were getting ready to go out so we could hear Mitch and Billy laughing while they were getting ready. Mitch had a *good* laugh.

He came back in and we all watched the *Big Brother* final – it was between Rylan, Heidi and Spencer. Then we all went out to the club.

We got to the venue and we were drinking and having a laugh. I had to stand for pictures with the people in the club who were all queuing, waiting to meet me. I was wondering where Mitch had got to when all of a sudden I saw him – there he was at the end of the queue! He walked over to me all casually and said, 'Can I get a kiss?'

We kissed and it was amazing. Standing in line for me was the sweetest thing anyone had ever done. The best part is that we got a picture of it.

I was buzzing.

Then we both got really drunk and lost each other.

En route back to the hotel, Melissa was trying to get me up the stairs and accidentally pushed me into a wall, which gave me a massive egg on my head. We got back to the room and heard Billy next door with some girl – but we'd lost Mitch. The next morning, the phone rang. It was the manager of the hotel.

'Have you lost your friend? He's asleep downstairs.'

Mitch was exactly like me!

The next thing we hear is Mitch banging on the door. He'd got so drunk he ended up sleeping in the reception of the hotel. He climbed into bed with me and Melissa and started showing us funny videos. It was a strange morning, but still very lovely.

By the time he and Billy left, we'd become Facebook friends but he still wasn't following me on Twitter. I messaged him my number and I waited all day for a text. I couldn't stop looking at my phone. I had to go to Scotland next for a PA and on the way there I turned to Melissa and said, 'This is the man I'm going to marry.'

I liked him so much. I couldn't stop staring at my phone. Where was he?! He texted me after a few hours and it was full of loads of different emojis. I waited another few hours before I replied (we were both trying to play it cool).

We started seeing each other a lot after that – he'd come and meet me when I had a PA or I was in London doing press. But we'd only ever meet up in hotels. I didn't go to his and he didn't come to mine because I lived so far away. I didn't want to meet his parents until I knew it was serious. He was the first proper boyfriend I'd had since being in *Geordie Shore* and I was worried about meeting his mum and dad because of them having seen me in the show. I thought, 'What are they going to do when they meet me?' I was convinced they'd have a bad impression of me from the telly and wouldn't like me and it would make me feel crap and insecure. So the only time we'd see each other was in hotels; we didn't even go out for food. I always used to say, 'Your mam and dad must think I'm awful.' I was so worried about it. He'd try and convince me they didn't but I knew they did.

We waited about three weeks before we had sex. I really liked him and I was a bit nervous. We did it for the first time on Valentine's Day.

I still had bright blonde hair and I managed to get all my makeup really nice. I remember thinking I looked dead good so I took loads of selfies beforehand. Then I said to him, 'Let's get some alcohol,' so we went to the shop and I got wine and he got vodka. Back in the hotel room we were downing our drinks a bit too quickly and ended up getting really pissed. Then we went to have sex and . . . let's just say fireworks didn't exactly go off that night (maybe there was just a small Catherine wheel).

Then the next time we did it was just before I went away to Australia on a PA tour and it was really, *really* good and I was thinking, 'Yes! Everything is working!'

Then something really funny happened. He was on top of me . . . he was just about to come and so was I . . . and he sneezed and a massive bogey came out of his nose! He was mortified and shouted, 'Oh my God, I've got a bogey!' and quickly hid his head and was trying to wipe his nose while still lying on top of me! I was trying to say, 'It's not bad!' but I was laughing so much that then he started laughing. Can you believe he had a bogey in the middle of

SEX just as the good part was about to happen?! It was hilarious. Poor Mitch.

Part of the reason I was able to spend so much time in London with Mitch was because Gary and me were filming an episode of Channel 5's *Celebrity Wedding Planner*. And what I haven't mentioned yet is that Mitch wasn't just Billy's friend . . . he was also mates with Gary. They'd all spent a summer in Malia together. And at this point Gary knew *nothing* about the fact I was seeing his friend.

Filming *Celebrity Wedding Planner* was such a laugh. Me and Gary were picking the craziest things, the couple we were working for were dead nice and we couldn't wait for them to see what we'd done. It took about a week to film in total and the days were really long; we had to juggle it all around PAs and *Geordie Shore* and it was quite full on. Usually if I ever did anything in London I'd get the train home. And Gary knew this.

One morning, I went to meet Gary at the bridal shop because we were picking the dress.

'Where have you come from?' asked Gary.

'I've come from London.'

'Why were you in London last night?'

'Oh, erm, I've been spending a lot of time in London.'

'Why?' He seemed really angry.

'Well, it's got nothing to do with you.'

'You've met someone?'

'Well, yeah, I might have.'

'Is it anyone I know?'

'Well . . . I don't know, you might know him.'

'Is it one of me fucking friends?'

'I don't think it's your friend.'

'Is it one of Billy's friends?'

'Yeah.'

'Is it Rob?'

'No.'

'Is it Shane?' He was getting really annoyed and was reeling through a list of names. I kept saying, 'No, no, no . . .'

In the end he said, 'Who is it then?'

'It's Mitch.'

'WHAT? You've been seeing Mitch?'

Instantly Gary started trying to put me off him. 'Well, you do realise he's just a lad like me, don't you? He goes out and shags all the time. You do realise he's like that, Charlotte, don't you?'

'Well, no, I didn't realise that . . .' I muttered. 'But it's not like I'm boyfriend and girlfriend with him.' I didn't know what to say.

Then Gary's mood suddenly switched again. He was trying another tactic.

'Actually, he'll probably just get loved up with you. That's exactly what he did in Malia . . . he got loved up with a girl and didn't bother coming out because that's what he does. And actually also . . . his ex-girlfriend was *really* nice.'

He'd gone from trying to put me off him to making me want to be jealous!

'Whatever,' I shrugged.

Gary didn't speak to me for the rest of the day.

I have to admit, despite the fact I was falling for Mitch, I did like Gary's reaction. It proved he was bothered and he hates showing that. I had a little laugh to myself and thought, 'Yes, I've got one over on you!'

It was just before we started series six, when we went over to Australia on a PA tour, that I decided I really, *really* liked Mitch. I invited him to come over there with me and that's when we grew properly close. But we said we weren't going to make it official because we'd only just met and I was about to spend seven weeks on the other side of the world (series six of *Geordie Shore* was also in Australia) and you can't jump into something that quick when you have that much of a commitment ahead of you.

But because of my feelings for Mitch, throughout the whole of series six of *Geordie Shore* I was officially the most boring person on TV *ever*. Still, there was one upside at least – the way I felt about Mitch meant that by the time we started filming I had totally shaken off the whole Gary spell.

Shazam!

17

G'DAY AND G'BYE

When I got to Australia for series six, I wasn't the same Charlotte. I should've been bouncing off the walls with excitement about the fact we were filming a whole series in Oz. But from the minute I landed, all I thought about was Mitch and how much I *hated* being away from him. I was being so boring. But I was IN LOVE. I changed my hair colour back to brown, too; I wanted to be back to my old self. I didn't want to be blonde any more – I needed to wash Gary out of my head!

We're not allowed our mobile phones during filming and

it can be hard not having any contact with the outside world. I didn't know what Mitch was doing or where he was. On a Friday and Saturday, I'd think, 'He's going out now.' I hated it.

Right from the start, Mitch made it clear to me that he didn't want to be on camera, which meant I couldn't call him during filming.

So, do you know what I did?

Halfway through the series, I bought a sneaky phone in a garage with a SIM card and after that I kept it with me but always had it on silent. The phone was so shit that the battery lasted ages; I put about $50 on it and it meant I could sneakily text Mitch without anyone knowing. I'd go into the toilet and whenever I pressed 'send' I'd flush the chain. I'd send him messages like, 'I miss you so much, I hate being apart,' and he'd reply, 'I miss you too, I can't wait to spend so much time together when you get back.'

That's when I knew it was real.

Gary could tell straight away that something had changed in me. He kept asking me to have a chat – it must've felt weird for him not getting my attention 24/7 – but when I looked at him I just felt empty inside. I felt nothing; it was like I was a starfish, just a shape with no feelings.

He wasn't the only one to notice I was different. I wasn't in the mood to get mortal every night, and Vicky – who was now very single, having finally split with Ricci – started moaning at me and saying I was being boring. I told her, 'If being mature equals boring, then I'm not bothered!'

I spent a lot of time in series six crying over Mitch. I was worried he might not trust me and think I'd do something with Gary. And with my track record, I couldn't blame him.

To celebrate the fact I had the willpower to stay away from Gary, I also got my first tattoo. It's a symbol that means Power, Love and Peace and it's on my wrist. I'd copied it off a girl I followed on Instagram and loved the fact it summed up everything I felt. I had willPOWER. I was falling in LOVE with someone else and I was at PEACE. I never told Gary it was to do with him; he'd think it was something to boast about.

I knew I wasn't being me, but I couldn't help myself. I did *try* and be more sociable one night and downed loads of shots in an attempt to resurrect 'Fun Charlotte' but I just ended up being sick all over the tables, rolling around on the floor and then pissing on the sofa back at the villa. I seriously think I might have a medical problem! (I didn't tell anyone until the next morning, and by that time Scott had already shagged on it. Oh well.)

Despite my grumbling over Mitch, we did loads of fun stuff while we were in Oz. We went white water rafting – although that made me feel like I was back in the womb and mum was giving birth to me again. We also went on a trip to see some dolphins and it was the best day of my life – better than the day I got my period and felt like a woman. I love dolphins; they're such wonderful, intelligent creatures. And they're the only other animals that have sex for pleasure. We also celebrated that famous Australian national day, Grilled Cheese Sandwich Day, and to me, any nation that devotes a single day to a grilled cheese sandwich is the kind of nation I want to be born in.

Here are the days I think should be celebrated:

- Apple Days (I like a Cox's apple best and they're very British)
- Help an Old Person Day
- Be Kind on Social Media Day
- Cheat Days (so I can eat what I like)

Sophie's boyfriend Joel came out to visit her in Oz (and woke us up one morning banging pots and pans in our faces, which was nice) and that just made me miss Mitch more. I kept thinking how I'd love him to be in Australia with us, hanging out and cooking breakfast with the lads; I knew he would get on with everyone so well.

James had got all serious with a girl called Kate and he managed to get her over for a holiday.

Watching everyone being all loved-up got too much in the end. I started crying constantly again and I felt devastated – I missed Mitch so much it was actually making me want to leave Australia. I just didn't want to be there any more. Do I follow my head or my heart? How are you supposed to know what to do in situations like that?

Around this time, me, Vicky, Gary and Holly went on a trip to the outback, also known as the bush (ha ha). It was spooky at first because we turned up in the middle of nowhere and we were told that when you go to the toilet out in the wild a frog could climb up your bum hole. It was so pitch black at night time that I could hardly see my own hand. I kept thinking, 'I bet there's a murderer here!'

We all sat by a fire listening to this man playing songs on his guitar, getting pissed and roasting marshmallows, and it was actually really nice. Proper 'back to nature' stuff. The four of us got a bit sentimental and started reminiscing and it was a nice change from hanging out in nightclubs. We were all sharing tents – me and Holly, Vicky and Gary (there was something going on between them in that series, I'm sure of it – they were really flirting but I didn't care about Gary any more, so what the hell). I hardly got any sleep though because I was worried we might be eaten by bears.

The next day I *actually* spoke to Mitch on the phone – it was filmed on camera but you couldn't hear what he was saying on the other end so Mitch was OK. Talking to him and having his reassurance put everything back into perspective and I knew I needed to stay. This was an amazing experience I'd been given and I'd have been a tit to leave.

We went horse riding while we were still in the outback and seeing Gary looking all scared on this lovely animal made me laugh my head off. I looked at him and just thought he was pathetic and ugly (whereas I'm obviously good at riding anything!).

Meanwhile, back at the villa, we all had an 'anger management' session. This woman went round asking us all questions one by one in front of each other and I admitted I used to get angry with Gary. I said he used to pretend he cared about me but he clearly *didn't*; I was griefing him in front of his face while everyone else was watching. It was actually quite therapeutic! He hated it. Then I told her that sometimes I got bored during sex with him and Gary hid behind a cushion.

I'm not sure if it was spurred on by our therapy session or not, but by the end of this series, Gary and I finally opened up about all the stuff we'd never spoken about. He confessed to me that he'd played with my emotions (I'd been waiting for the apology for so long!), while I told him I would never ever forgive him for what he did and that he had lost me a long time ago.

But the strangest development was when I ended up asking *Gary* for advice about *Mitch*! I told him I was worried that having been away from him for so long, it might not be the same when I got back. And wise ol' Gary told me that if I felt that strongly about him then it would be fine. It was probably one of the nicest moments I'd had with Gary in a long time.

Just before the end of the series, James and Gary had a huge fight and had to be split up by the crew. There had been issues brewing between them for ages – James was in a different place to where he used to be because of Kate and he now thought Gary was a cocky idiot who only cared about himself. In the end, the pair of them were sent away as punishment and only came back right before we had to return home. At one point I thought Gary had left without saying goodbye and that was quite sad. This trip had signified the end of an era between the two of us and I was a bit disappointed to think that our last days would be so crap and uneventful.

What I didn't know was that Gary had written me a note. He'd poured his heart out and finally shown some emotion, telling me how he thought and felt about me. He'd hidden it in my makeup bag and only let Sophie know where it was. Sophie read it then told me about it. She said it was three paragraphs long and that the punctuality was shit (I think she meant punctuation). She said I'd cry when I read it, which made me feel apprehensive. Was he trying to mess with my head again? Did I even want to know

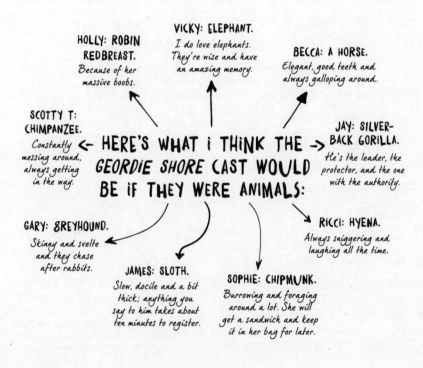

HOLLY: ROBIN REDBREAST.
Because of her massive boobs.

VICKY: ELEPHANT.
I do love elephants. They're wise and have an amazing memory.

BECCA: A HORSE.
Elegant, good teeth and always galloping around.

SCOTTY T: CHIMPANZEE.
Constantly messing around, always getting in the way.

HERE'S WHAT I THINK THE GEORDIE SHORE CAST WOULD BE IF THEY WERE ANIMALS:

JAY: SILVER-BACK GORILLA.
He's the leader, the protector, and the one with the authority.

GARY: GREYHOUND.
Skinny and svelte and they chase after rabbits.

JAMES: SLOTH.
Slow, docile and a bit thick; anything you say to him takes about ten minutes to register.

SOPHIE: CHIPMUNK.
Burrowing and foraging around a lot. She will get a sandwich and keep it in her bag for later.

RICCI: HYENA.
Always sniggering and laughing all the time.

what he had to say after all this time? I was dreading it. The next morning I saw the letter folded up in my makeup bag but I genuinely didn't know how it was going to make me feel. I said to myself, 'Do I want to have taken all these steps forward just to go back again?'

Nothing he could say now would change anything. So I ripped it up.

In the end, just as I was about to leave to get on the plane, Gary suddenly came back to the villa. He told me that his best times and memories have been in *Geordie Shore* with me and that if Mitch gets to experience anything like that then he's a lucky guy. We had a cuddle. It was all quite touching. As I got in the taxi for the airport, I knew I wasn't just leaving Gary there, I was leaving 'Charlotte and Gary' for good.

MARNIE: BLACK PANTHER.

Not as soft as a cat but very affirmative, if you saw a panther walking along you'd stop and stare. She gets all the attention and is very majestic.

CHLOE: AN OSTRICH IN A FUNNY HAT.

You don't even know what she is. Flapping her wings everywhere and not being able to walk properly, but in a funny way.

AND THE NEWBIES...

NATHAN: A LION.

Fierce!

KYLE: PIGEON.

Has a bad nose - a beak, a bit like me. Kyle and me would be pigeons and we'd fly everywhere and eat crumbs off the floor.

AARON: A PERSIAN CAT.

Soft natured and pristine. He wears the most amazing clothes and cats are dead clean and graceful.

18

PLEASE DO NOT SWEAR...
OR WET THE BED ON LIVE TV

MY CELEB BIG BROTHER HOUSEMATES

Danielle Marr: Some woman who was meant to be famous in Ireland. I'd never heard of her and nor had anyone else – she was out first

Ron Atkinson: Football agent who I pretended was my granddad

Sophie Anderton: Pretty model who spoke about herself a lot

Dustin Diamond: Played Screech in *Saved by the Bell* and was nowhere near as fun as I hoped

Bruce Jones: Actor who played Les Battersby in *Coronation Street*

Vicky Entwistle: Actress who played Janice Battersby in *Coronation Street* – didn't like her

Courtney Stodden: American model *Playboy*-type person who was always on the *Mail* Online, had massive boobs and was married to some rich fella who was much older than her

Louie Spence: Dancer and TV star from Pineapple Dance Studios and *Dancing on Ice*. Hilarious funny man

Mario Falcone: Starred in *The Only Way Is Essex* and was always cheating on his girlfriend Lucy and denying it

Carol McGiffin: Presenter on *Loose Women* and journalist. Very witty

Lauren Harries: TV personality who used to be a boy and was once into antiques and appeared on a show with Terry Wogan

Abz Love: The quiet one from 5ive who now lives on a farm or something

Celebrity Big Brother was something that *everyone* in *Geordie Shore* wanted to do and for a long while a lot of the cast had been giving it the big talk, saying things like, 'I don't need you lot. I've been asked to go on *Big Brother*!'

There was one time I'll never forget, when we were filming series three of *Geordie Shore* in Mexico and Vicky got really drunk and started screaming, 'I don't have to be here and put up with this shit, I've been asked to be on *Big Brother*!' She was totally loving herself. We were all sitting there thinking, 'Eh? There's no way she's been asked to be on that!' But at one point or another, everyone in the *Geordie Shore* house had the *Big Brother* rant. For a while Gary did it too. He was talking about going into *Big Brother* for *so long* but it never actually happened.

The interview was similar to the one I had with the *Geordie Shore* producers. 'What's your craziest moment? What's the funniest thing that's ever happened to you? What was your most embarrassing moment? What's your favourite kind of people? Who would you *not* like to live with?'

And the reaction was the same too. Once again, the producers didn't believe a word I was saying! What the hell? I couldn't believe this was happening again.

'Do you seriously mean to say that you would actually be the same kind of person in *Big Brother* as you are in *Geordie Shore*?'

'What did you think I was doing in that house? Making it all up?'

'Really? You actually wee yourself?'

'Yeah, when I get too drunk I wee meself.'

My agent Kate was sitting in the interview with me and she was laughing. She laughs a lot when I'm talking.

I never ever got excited about going on the show because I don't like to get my hopes up about anything. So I didn't ever let myself think it was a big deal. It got closer and closer and I still didn't tell a soul.

And then it was confirmed. I was put in hiding for three days before I entered the house; I was in a room with no phone and no telly. Whenever I had to leave to go and do our pre-*Big Brother* interviews I had to have a towel over my head. It was weird but it was really exciting.

I had a chaperone called Lisa and she was lovely, we had such a laugh. I can't imagine being stuck in there on my own; I think I'd have cried my eyes out.

The day we went in I was shaking like a leaf. I stood behind the giant eye on the stage thinking, 'What the fuck am I actually doing?' and when you're behind the eye you can't even hear whether people are cheering you or not, it's all quiet. All that's going through you is adrenaline.

The eye door opened and I was overwhelmed with cheers. Phew. I was wearing the most awful outfit because I was really fat at the time, so I would only ever dress to be comfortable. I had these frilly ankle socks on as if I was a twelve-year-old and had been dressed to go to school by me mam, some black manly boots with buckles on and a big baggy skirt and top.

I'll always remember the reaction I got after walking over to meet Emma Willis. I said to her, 'I'm so scared, I'm shitting myself,' and she looked at me really weirdly. I instantly felt like she didn't like me. It was as if she was looking down on me, thinking, 'Who's this idiot from *Geordie Shore*?'

I think I grew on her in the end, though. I feel like I grow on a lot of people when I'm forced into their lives.

I reckon I grew on Emma Willis in the same way I grew on Holly Willoughby. I remember sitting on the panel of *Celebrity Juice* with Holly and she said, 'So is your mum OK with everything you do on telly?' and I replied, 'Well, it's not like I'm murdering anyone,' at which she looked totally disapproving. It's always the women on TV with children who feel like that about me. They can't get their head around what I get up to on *Geordie Shore* and they obviously think, 'If that was my child . . .'

Being totally honest, it always makes me feel a bit shit. It makes me feel belittled because they're such high-up, sought-after people and to know they're thinking that isn't nice. But I won Holly round in the end. I did *Celebrity Juice* about three times and then I went on *This Morning* so regularly that it got to the point where she would come to my dressing room and say 'hi' and that's when I *knew* she liked me.

Anyway, after I'd been introduced to the crowd, I walked down the *Big Brother* staircase and I thought, 'Shit, the house is small! It looks much bigger on telly but it's really titchy and confined.' Everything always seems bigger on TV – studios, houses, even people.

Vicky and Bruce from *Coronation Street* were already in there, so was Abz from 5ive and Courtney Stodden. The first thing I thought was, 'Oh my God, it's that girl who's always on the *Mail* Online' – to me, Courtney was the most famous person out of the lot of them.

I thought Vicky was a bitch straight away. I went to top up my glass of wine and she pulled a face and said, 'You can't do that, *everyone's* got to have a glass.'

I was excited to meet Dustin because I loved *Saved by the Bell* and he played Screech, but he turned out to be a bit of a weirdo. Sometimes it's not good to meet your idols; they let you down. I'd never met Mario from *TOWIE* before but we became really good friends; he was like my brother in there.

I liked Courtney a lot. On the first night we got on dead well and I helped her sew her toy bunny up because the beads were coming out of its bum hole. Her figure was unbelievable – how could any human being have a body like that?

She had a husband who was loads older than her and she'd talk about him all the time but I never wanted to ask too many questions in case I seemed rude or nosy – I'd just lurk around listening when other people were asking them instead (that way I still got the answers!).

Waking up in that house that first morning, I felt really insecure. I walked to the kitchen and thought: 'I can't go on if I'm going to feel like this.' It felt like the first day at school again – I didn't know anyone and didn't know who to go over to. I was so scared, it was awful. I thought, 'I am literally *no one* compared to these people. Mario is on

Me and the crew on the edge of the ice floe, filming The Charlotte Crosby Experience. They were an amazing team.

The elephant that brought me to tears.

I loved dressing up while exploring different cultures.

But I was never really comfortable in the geisha attire!

India had by far the prettiest clothes!

My best friends from home. Me and these girls have had wilder nights than you'll ever see on Geordie Shore.

Me and Melissa with Adam and Jamie. My work colleagues, and now best friends. I love them so much.

Team photo after a Nostalgia shoot!

Me and Mitch sunbathing
in his garden.

Me and my trainers: Richard (below) and David (Right). We always mess around when we are together.

Feeling proud at a DVD signing!

Fat Charlotte always haunted me.

Gracing the red carpet for the NTAs was amazing!

Me and Mitch looking smart.

We've come so far – with old faces and new, here we are promoting the TENTH SERIES of G Shore!

Doing press for my range Nostalgia!

such a big show on telly, Carol is from *Loose Women*, Ron Atkinson is lovely like a granddad and famous in the football world . . .' I was just on *Geordie Shore*!

I was frightened of Carol McGiffin to start with, too. I always thought she was quite hard-faced and straight-talking on *Loose Women*, and that's exactly what she was like in the house. She told me she'd heard that 'a slag from *Geordie Shore* is going into the house'. She didn't like me at first. But as I got to know her I realised she wasn't scary, she was a brilliant friend. I knew from the second day when I woke up that I wanted to be friends with her – she was a lot older and I thought she could stick up for me if I *did* ever get into a fight in there. She knew exactly what she was doing – baking, washing her clothes – and I never knew how to do any of that. So I started following her around the house a lot. I also learnt very quickly that she loves to get drunk and she'd say to me, 'Charlotte, what you do in *Geordie Shore* is nothing compared to what I used to get up to! If there were cameras on me, my mum would have kicked me out.' (I'm not sure she'd have wet the bed on telly though . . . I got really drunk one night quite early on in the show and woke up in a wet patch. Everyone was disgusted at me!)

Louie Spence, Lauren Harries and Sophie Anderton were also on the show but they'd been put into some place called 'The Temple' for the first three days, where they were making us do stuff without us knowing.

When they entered the house and I saw Lauren I got a

bit of a shock at first. Not because she was weird but just that everything about her was crazy. She had this massive blonde afro and she couldn't open her eyes because her eyelash extensions had been done so badly that it had glued her eyes shut. So you could never tell if she was looking at you or not. When she opened her eyes you could see they were really red and covered in pus. Two days in, me and Louie said to her, 'We're going to sort you out because you look horrendous,' and we took her eyelashes out really gently so they wouldn't hurt, soaked her eyes in warm water because they were so badly infected, then we took off all of her fake tan because it was patchy everywhere and we helped her straighten her hair. She looked a lot better afterwards but not for long.

She was such a funny character; she had the weirdest, most hilarious and totally made-up stories. None of us believed any of them were real but she didn't realise as she'd convinced herself they were all *totally* true. In one of the stories she said she was in the car with her family and her nana was driving along the motorway and pushed Lauren out of the car. She told us that no one realised she wasn't in the car until about fifteen minutes later when they said, 'Oh, where's Lauren?' and they looked out of the car window to see her hanging onto the tyre being dragged along the road! Obviously that was *not* true. There was another story about a friend of Lauren's who wasn't really a friend but she just used to want Lauren's nice things – antiques and stuff – and one day they were sitting in the car playing with something when this friend took the handbrake off and they rolled into a lake! Her stories were very odd but very funny.

Louie Spence was such a character, too. He was happy and crazy most of the time but there were some occasions when he would go into quiet mode and would sit by himself and stare into space. He would do it for hours and you'd think he was in a bad mood. You'd try to speak to him and he'd just give you one-word answers. I remember at one point me and Carol said to *Big Brother*, 'He's literally sapping the energy out of the room,' but when I got out of the house, me mam and dad said, 'We never understood why you and Carol would say Louie was an energy-sapper?' Turned out they didn't show much of that on telly so we must've looked like we were just moaning about nothing. He had a lot going on in his life though so I think that was why he was very down sometimes. The majority of the time he's fun and dancing around and is the *funniest* person I've ever met – he made me laugh so much. I made three really good mates in there and it was him, Carol and Mario.

Sophie Anderton was a really nice girl but she was very self-obsessed. I guess she used to be a supermodel so it's only right that she would be pretty keen on herself! If you said something she would butt in and say she knew better or she knew someone who'd done it first. Every conversation came back to her. I don't think she realised she was doing it though so she was harmless.

Mario went in the house with a bad reputation as a

womaniser because he'd cheated on his girlfriend Lucy so much. He talked about how much he loved Lucy but I think he was in denial and was just saying it because it made himself sound better. I don't think that's how he genuinely felt.

On day three we all had to participate in a task called 'Guess What?' For this task, housemates had to reveal three stories about themselves to the rest of the group. Once a housemate had revealed their three stories, the rest of the group had to pick what they thought the viewers would select as the 'most interesting'. The more stories they guessed correctly as the 'most interesting', the more prizes the house-mates won. It was a horrible task because my category was about me having sex on TV. I had to read mine out and Sophie Anderton said, 'Oh no, Big Brother! That's so harsh, how could you write such a horrible thing about the girl?' – she thought the producers had made up a story about me! 'Oh, er, it's true,' I told her, feeling really awkward. I know I say I don't care what people say about me but when it's in your face right in front of you and they're disapproving, it's hard not to be at least a bit affected. One of Carol's stories was that she'd been celibate for years and I was dead shocked. But then she explained it afterwards and said it was because she'd lost her mam and it put her off doing anything like that. I wonder what it must be like to go without sex? I think maybe I could do it for about eight months. Not a year, that would be too much. Someone said it's meant to do things to your brain but I thought it would affect you down *there*.

Some of the tasks were genius, though. There was one called 'Busk Brother', where each celebrity had to showcase his or her talent in the garden. Each housemate was given a money bag with three gold coins and when you did a performance you had to put your money bag out in front of you so the others could give you one of their coins if they thought you were any good. Somehow or other I ended up winning the task because I got the most coins and I won a burger and some chips as a reward! I'd acted out a scene from *Geordie Shore*; I pretended I was on a night out and put a hairpiece in so I could act as if I was Vicky. I'd made some makeshift sick by mixing milk, cereal, and tomato sauce all in a glass. I danced in my imaginary club, doing slut-drops then went to take a swig from the glass – which looked like alcohol – but was really my pretend puke. I was 'sick' all over myself and then went home and passed out on the doorstep. And everyone found it really funny.

Another time there was a 'Random Task Generator Machine' and Mario had to slow-dance wearing a mankini. He had his hand over his penis the whole time because he thought it was going to look so small!

There was also a 'dance-off' competition and Mario and me had to do hip-hop. But I'll always remember Carol doing an interpretive dance dressed in this massive leotard. She had to move about without speaking and I couldn't stop laughing.

I didn't mind the punishments, to be honest; I found them quite funny. Mario and I got told off for drawing over some of the housemates' faces on the memory wall and, as a punishment for doing so, we had to draw over each other's actual faces and stay like it until further notice. We'd drawn willies and penises on people's heads so we just drew them all over each other too!

For another shopping task, Carol, Lauren and Mario were kept as fake 'prisoners'. Their mission was to pretend to be prisoners while actually living in luxury. Meanwhile the rest of us had to perform a series of demands that would enable their 'release'. We had to eat 'prison food' of chicken feet and pigs' ears – it all tasted disgusting but because it was Carol and Mario, Louie and I were desperate to get them out. I was sick all over the plate once but we would have done *anything*.

Afterwards it was revealed it was all just a trick, but Carol and Mario told us, 'There was nothing luxurious about being down there!' They were in a room below the house with no natural light and were stuck there for hours with nowhere to go.

You might be wondering why I haven't so much as breathed a word about Abz. But that's because I hardly noticed him in the house for the first couple of weeks! He was so quiet and he made people feel like he didn't want them to talk to him, so you felt a bit uncomfortable going over and starting any conversation in case he blanked you. I didn't feel that he liked me at all and kept saying so in the diary room, so they handcuffed us together and we had to spend the whole day like that. We eventually ended up finding stuff to talk about, which was clearly the point of the exercise.

We were all sent letters from home and some of the housemates had to choose who needed them most out of the people handcuffed together. They decided that Abz needed his more than I did so mine got shredded. I was really angry at first. I lay on the bed crying because all I could think was that I wanted to hear from me mam and dad. The others told me that I had friends in the house and didn't need it but I felt like I was getting penalised for being the youngest. I got to read Carol's out to her, though, which made me really happy – I was crying when I read it! She'd been saying how she thought her fiancé Mark wasn't going to be there for her when she came out because she'd been embarrassing herself but he wrote such loving things and said, 'I'm still here.' It was so cute.

I didn't think about what was going on in the outside world until Vanessa Feltz came in as part of a task. She had to deliver the viewers' thoughts and opinions. She told us all the horrible things people had said about all of us, apart from Lauren – she just seemed to have amazing comments. She said I was a disgusting excuse for a girl, weeing myself on national TV, and that people were saying they didn't know how my parents could put up with me. I got really upset. I normally try not to care what people say but that house does funny things to you – you've got nothing else to think about while you're in there, so the littlest things get to you. It was especially bad hearing that people were saying I was the worst one compared to everyone else! Even though I knew we were being filmed in there, it wasn't the same as in *Geordie Shore* where the camera crew are right next to you. You can't see them behind the mirrors so it was easy to forget what you were doing or how you were coming across.

We were all convinced that Lauren was going to win. Not only did Vanessa give her the best public feedback, but the cheers she used to get on eviction nights were so loud. There was no way it wouldn't be her.

Bit on the Side presenter Rylan Clark entered the house for the day in another task. He came in the day after I'd had a massive row with Vicky. There had been a rumour that Lauren had got to see her mam in the diary room in secret and I got annoyed about it, which led to me and Vicky having a big argument during which she called me a 'fat Geordie slag'. So when Rylan came in, he could sense there was an atmosphere. He was really sweet to me and I started crying. Vicky and I made up afterwards but I still didn't like her.

I thought about Mitch all the time when I was in the house, but luckily we were only in there for three weeks, which was nothing compared to being in Australia for seven weeks for *Geordie Shore*. I drew a matchstick person on my wall to remind me of Mitch and made sure it had his big penis.

Louie was the seventh celebrity to get evicted from the house – he went after Courtney and I was *shocked*. How

could someone who'd kept me laughing from start to finish have been sent out by the public before Vicky who was a bitch and before Abz who was boring? I was so pissed off. When Carol left I was also really fucked off but then all of a sudden it was me, Abz and Lauren and then Lauren got the boot and I thought, 'EH?'

I was so confused.

It had to be Abz.

When Emma said I was the winner, I thought, 'What the Actual Fuck?' I couldn't believe it. I was so happy that I'd won and I kept thinking about *Geordie Shore* and all the negative comments we'd had in the past and that now I'd been on this show I'd proved that we weren't so bad after all. We'd got such a bad name in the press and I felt finally

I'd shown everyone we were good people! I was so excited at the thought of seeing Mitch and me mam and dad until I started thinking, 'Oh no, is Mitch going to still want to be with me?' Everyone who had a partner in the house got worried about that at some point or other.

I didn't have a very dramatic exit, mind you. It wasn't a very good one. The smoke machine had gone crazy so it was firing out from all cylinders, meaning no one could see me coming down the steps and I couldn't see where I was walking. I just about made out a cloud that looked like Mitch and he looked so handsome I wanted to kiss him and then I saw a shape that looked a bit like Mam and Dad! I just wanted to get home and give them all the biggest cuddle.

From that moment, having been crowned the winner of *Celebrity Big Brother* 2013, it really felt like my life had changed. I suddenly started to get invited on shows I'd never been asked on before and was getting all sorts of offers. One of them was to do my very own TV show visiting places around the world . . .

19

CHARLOTTE COLUMBUS

My TV show was called *The Charlotte Crosby Experience* and it was made by a great production company called Rumpus for a channel called TLC. I couldn't believe I had been given my own show – just me, exploring different parts of the world! But as amazing as it was to get offered such a gig like that, I knew it was a double-edged sword – what if no one watched it? What if wasn't a success?

As I've said, I think I can be a pretty pessimistic person – I never want to get my hopes up just so I don't get disappointed. But if I'm honest I did get a bit overexcited about this show and I did allow myself to think it could do well. I knew how much the TV channel had put into it. TLC really believed in me and they had invested a lot of money into this show. No pressure or anything . . .

I was sent to four different places – Japan, India, Canada and the Arctic Circle – to experience their cultures and see what life was like away from the nightclubs of *Geordie Shore*. But to be honest, despite all the amazing things I saw and did, I was quite preoccupied with my life behind the scenes. Since my success in *Big Brother* I'd been so busy that Mitch and I had spent hardly any time together, and it was taking its toll on us. We were arguing more than we'd ever argued and our relationship was breaking down. Whereas before we'd been fighting about me being on *Geordie Shore*, this time it was the distance that was killing us. I was on the other side of the world and every time we tried to talk I was either going to bed and he was going out or he was at work so he couldn't really speak. Everything was annoying me – especially when I had a day off and he'd be going out with his friends on a night out. It was all getting too much.

I remember being in India and just feeling so down. I was on the other side of the world, I had to fly straight to Australia afterwards for PA work and I wasn't connecting with Mitch at all. Every time we spoke on the phone it would end up in a row. Meanwhile I was trying to make a TV show where I was going to this royal Indian wedding. I couldn't even hold my own relationship together, so how could I pretend to be all happy for someone else? The only reason I was remotely excited about being in India was because I thought I might get to ride an elephant.

I was sent to live with an Indian family in this huge palace. We'd been filming all day. I'd been on a plane, filming with people showing me how I was meant to behave at a posh wedding (I even had to walk with a book on my head at one point!), and by the time we arrived it was midnight and I had to walk into the palace with the cameras following behind me. I entered to be greeted by a swarm of about 150 people – no word of a lie. I felt so intimidated and shy but I knew I had to perform for the camera. We'd started shooting at 9 a.m. and we didn't finish until 4 a.m. the next day because the Indian family didn't want to stop partying. I know I'm usually out doing that on *Geordie Shore* but at least then I have Jägerbombs to keep me going. I take my hat off to anyone who has their own show and does stuff like that to camera all the time – it's hard work with no one to bounce off!

That first night in the palace was really hard and I got quite emotional. After I'd finished filming I sat in the bedroom and cried. I really didn't want to be there. There wasn't even Wi-Fi! I felt like a spoilt brat but I was just so lonely. And I was worried about what was happening back home with Mitch.

Thankfully I felt a bit better the next day and the Indian wedding was beautiful. I was told that seventy per cent of Indian marriages are arranged ones (not sure if that's true so don't quote me in any exams). God, I wouldn't let me mam pick my clothes let alone the man I would spend the rest of my life with – what if he had a small penis? The palace looked so pretty, it was like a rainbow had been sick everywhere but in the most amazing way. Putting on a sari was so difficult, though; I got into a right mess. God knows how the hell they do that every morning. I'd never make it out the door.

And it was because of one of those saris that I nearly didn't make it out of there alive (well, I nearly lost an arm anyway . . . kind of). I'd been up for sixteen hours and I'd been in a sari all day, I was tired and had my flip flops on and I was meant to hold the material of the sari in my hand every time I walked so I didn't trip up. The bedroom I was in was miles away from anything – there wasn't a mini bar or fridge – so if you wanted some water you had to walk all the way to the kitchen, which was on the other end of the courtyard, pour yourself a drink and take it back to your room. So off I went to get one and on the way back I was walking down the staircase, water in one hand and a fan in the other (it was hot!), but because I didn't own three hands there was no way I could also keep hold of my sari.

I think you know where this is heading . . .

I was walking down the stone staircase and I slipped . . . and my sari got stuck. I had two arms full of bangles – jewellery is a big thing in India – and as I fell and the glass smashed everywhere, the bangles cut into my skin and I had a massive flesh wound on my arm. The cut was wide open and there was blood everywhere. I'd smacked my body right down the stairs. One of the Indian women started shouting, 'She needs to go to hospital!' and at that I just fainted. When I came round again, this Indian man was wrapping my arm up so tightly that I couldn't feel anything. One of the camera crew was saying to him that he needed to be careful it didn't cut off my circulation, but because he was speaking in English the man didn't understand and carried on. The crew were more shaken than me and wanted me to get medical attention immediately but I told them I definitely didn't want to go to hospital – I was too scared. Besides, I knew I was flying to Australia from there so I could be seen by a doctor when I got there if it wasn't any better. In the end, I got on the plane with an arm that was oozing pus and by the time I arrived in Oz I was told I'd been stupid not to have had stitches immediately. But by then it was too late because it had started to heal so they had to leave my arm a gammy mess.

Before I left I did get a chance to see one of my dream animals – an elephant! I walked through the village asking people if they'd seen one and I saw a woman making stuff out of elephant poo. The search seemed to go on for ages but eventually I spotted one in the distance and the sight of it took my breath away. I burst into tears on the spot and was so overwhelmed. I think I must have been due for my period. I had no feelings but utter joy and love. I can imagine the only time I'll get that feeling is when I have a child. I even got to sit on the elephant – I was elephant woman! He was the third animal I'd ever cried at – the first time was when my fish Egg died and the second was when we filmed *Celebrity Wedding Planner* and we got an owl to bring the ring down the aisle to the bride.

As well as being home to the amazing elephant, India taught me that family is so important. They are so family-orientated and always have them around. Sometimes I feel like families can lose touch with each other but in India they are very loving.

Japan was the next place I visited. The thing I really noticed about the Japanese is that they keep their culture and traditions alive whereas sometimes I think British people lose sight of our roots and things we believe in, which is a shame. We let things slip a bit. But Japan was a difficult trip, too. I couldn't eat anything because the food was so disgusting – I didn't like sushi and I didn't like the weird noodles that they had. Everything was fishy and it made me feel sick.

I found this message in my memory book the other day – it was me writing to myself about all the things I still wanted to do in life and one of them included tasting sushi for the first time. Well, that was a disappointment!

I had to dress up in a geisha outfit and I looked awful. I must have been pulling such bad faces that the director had to take me aside and tell me off – he said I was acting like I wasn't being accepting of the Japanese culture, which was rude. I felt bad after that.

I was sent to 'Zen lessons' and told this would clear my mind. When you can't concentrate you call a man over and he whacks you with a stick – bit of a weird concept but there you go. Then we went to a 'cuddle café' where people literally pay to go in and hug women who are dressed in bunny outfits (not the sexy Hugh Hefner ones – these are more like onesies with ears). I was meant to be one of the bunnies but I found it all way too weird. A man came to try and hug me and I told him I'd shake his hand but that was it.

I did introduce the geisha girls to a game of 'I have never' though – it was hilarious. I told them they had to have a drink of tea if they had done any of the things I said.

'I have never had a wee outside.'

They both drank!

'I have never flashed my bum.'

They both drank again!

Maybe the Japanese weren't as sheltered as I thought!

Next I went to the Arctic Circle, which was so cold I was worried my clitoris would fall off. The extreme conditions were scary – we had to have safety briefings every single day telling us that when we went outside we had to make sure every single part of our skin was covered up because it was so cold that if you had your skin exposed for any longer than twenty seconds you'd get frost-bite straight away. The skin would turn brown or black and drop off. Most of the Inuits had loads of white patches on their face where they'd had frost-bite; it was like pigmentation in the skin.

It would get to the point where you'd be so cold that when you got home your neck scarf would just be ice. We built an igloo – after making them when it snowed in Newcastle it was something I'd always wanted to do for real – but the reality wasn't the same as my vision. It was hard work and I got bored after a while. I wasn't much help at all!

But it was a beautiful place and the amazing thing about the Inuits was that even though they don't have much they're so happy with their lot. They don't have any luxuries like us; they have to go out and hunt for food and make all their own clothes. But they proved to me you don't need a lot of materialistic things to be happy. There was also a brilliant old woman who I met and she really made me laugh, she reminded me of me nana and was so sarcastically funny it was hilarious. But the absolute best part of being in the Arctic was seeing polar bears. It was a once-in-a-lifetime experience and being so near them was the weirdest sensation. The men we were with were armed because the bears were so dangerous, but something inside me wanted them to get near just so I could see them properly. I didn't once get scared of them, I didn't think about the fact that if they came close they might eat me. All I thought was that it was the most beautiful experience and I didn't want it to end. I got all emotional looking at them and couldn't stop crying. So that was now animal number four I'd been in tears over! And I have to admit, the polar bear experience pooed all over meeting the elephant (sorry, elephant).

However, by far my biggest 'journey' of the whole series

(and I mean emotional one, not how far I had to fly) was my time with this religious community called the Hutterites in Canada.

All I knew about them was that they were a bit like the Amish community; they were a bit behind the times, didn't have all the technology that we had, wore old-fashioned clothes and didn't listen to the same music as us.

When I got there everything seemed fine at first (even though the outfits they wore and made me dress in were awful). But after we'd been there for about two days, I was filming a scene in this couple's house and suddenly there was a banging on the door. A man came walking in with a shedload of giant A3 sheets of paper under his arm. I looked at one and I could see they were printouts of me – there was a picture of me on the toilet asleep, there were pictures of me with barely any clothes on.

Why did they have all these photos?

The man told us angrily to turn off the camera and I sat there in the house while he started speaking to one of the producers.

'Who is this girl? Why did you lie to us? Is she a prostitute? She has sex on TV: is she a porn star?'

I could hear everything and by now he was shouting.

It turned out that someone in the community had a computer and had done some research about me – so obviously the vagina picture came up, a picture of me with my tits out in *Big Brother* emerged, all the *Geordie Shore* stuff about me having sex on TV . . .

I ran into the corridor and burst into tears. I said to one of the researchers, 'I can't do this! How can I film here with people who think that of me?'

I could hear the man screaming, 'We want her out now; she's bad for our community. We don't want her giving us a bad name. I don't want her around our children!'

I couldn't believe this was happening. One of the producers came in, saying, 'Charlotte, are you OK?'

'Well, no, how do you expect me to do any more filming here after hearing all of that?'

'We're sorting it out, don't worry.'

'No, please . . . I want to leave now, I need me mam, I don't want to be here. I can't believe they've spoken about me like that.'

We left the house and I rang me mam and burst into tears. I was crying my eyes out, I felt so humiliated. She wanted me to come home, but I'd only been there for two days and we had a whole episode to make. I knew we couldn't just pack it all in. I had a job to do.

The next day I had to go back to the house and face up to the people who had kicked us out. We weren't allowed to bring the camera in but I was mic'ed up, so the crew just recorded the audio. I remember watching the scene when it aired on telly – it was just a shot of the exterior of the house and you could hear our muffled voices from inside.

It was such a hard thing to do. I braced myself, took a deep breath and went in. I looked them all in the eyes and I began . . .

'How can you be so awful about someone? I'm a young girl and I've come into your house to learn about your way of life and you have made me feel *this* big. How would you feel if this was one of your daughters going to a place where she knew no one and someone was awful to her about her lifestyle and what she did and made her feel like an idiot?'

They were taken aback and immediately I could see they felt remorseful.

'We're so sorry, we didn't mean it, Charlotte. We'd love you to stay a bit longer and learn more about the community.'

It had been like a peacekeeping mission and I was the ambassador. And I'd done it – I'd forged a pact!

After that there were still some people in the community who would peer through their blinds when I walked past their houses, but most of them were fine. We went to a church ceremony and the leader of the church did this big speech saying, 'We have visitors here and I've heard that some people in the community are making them feel unwelcome. This is *not* the way of God, this is *not* what God talks about in the New Testament . . .' It was blatantly obvious he was talking about me and I went so red. I was sitting on one of the pews of the church and everyone started staring at me.

By the end of the trip the families all wrote me letters and it was actually really moving. One woman wrote: 'Charlotte, I cannot thank you enough for coming into our community and for opening up our eyes to the outside

213

world and not just these four walls. I am so sorry for how you were treated but it's taught a lot of us who maybe weren't abiding by the Bible and God's words truly, that we need to change our ways and that maybe we shouldn't be living here if we can't go by the Lord's good word. You coming into this community is what we all needed. I count my lucky stars and I feel like you were a blessing from God. Our guardian angel, you have changed a lot here.'

I cried when I read it. The note was amazing. But bloody hell – *that* was a turnaround, wasn't it?

Because of all the travelling, during the filming I ran up the biggest phone bill of my entire life. If I asked you to guess it now, you'd never ever know what it was.

Want me to tell you?

Ten grand! I nearly died when I saw that bill.

I was away for four weeks in different places in the world and then I was in Australia doing a PA tour. So that was two months'-worth of phone bills. When I saw the bill I was so shocked that I couldn't actually speak for an hour and a half. I didn't know what to do with myself. I felt like a person with a bad gambling addiction. It was like that was the end of my life.

But I didn't pay it in the end. My dad found out I hadn't been getting any texts to warn me that I was going over my tariff limit. So he complained. I had to pay some of it but Dad managed to get the rest back. Thank fuck for Gary! (My dad that is, not the other one.)

20

OVER (BUT NOT OUT)

I've learnt from me mam and dad not to have an unrealistic expectation of relationships – you can't be soppy and romantic all the time. Arguments can be good things – they can keep everything interesting! Once I heard this massive crashing and banging downstairs and Mam had ripped the curtain pole down in a fit of anger. She has these little outbursts then regrets it afterwards because she's the one who has to fix any damages. Me dad just walks away and leaves her to it because he knows what she's like. He's the calm one whereas she's really feisty. I think that's the key – to make sure you and your partner balance each other out. That's how it works.

I take after me mam; that's where Psycho Charlotte comes from. I get fits of rage and want to smash things up.

Oh, and when Mam and Dad fight she always pretends to pack her bags to leave, that's another one. But because she *always* does it, no one ever takes her seriously. She still has the capacity to ruin holidays, though. They went to Turkey recently and I got a text from Dad: 'Your mam tried to pack her bags again to come home last night. Me and Nathaniel calmed her down though so all's well.'

It's never big, serious arguments. They just bicker over things like if my dad has been out too much in the week and she's feeling left out.

Sadly, at this point, the arguments brewing between me and Mitch had turned from little things into big things. And nothing was going right.

We were on the brink of splitting up. We were fighting all the time and on one occasion I threatened to smash up all his trophies (he's won loads from doing motocross). That would have been so awful of me. There's a good reason I've got the nickname Psycho Charlotte!

Geordie Shore was probably the cause of my biggest fights with Mitch. He didn't want me to speak about him on the show, he didn't like me being in there and he didn't want to have anything to do with it at all. It made it so hard to be in a relationship when he was refusing to be a part of one of the biggest things in my life – the show was my job.

To be fair, he did appear in one episode in series seven – and it was a total catastrophe. We were going to London and Holly asked him if he'd come and surprise me but he didn't want to – he couldn't bear the idea of being on camera. He said he was embarrassed but I was hurt because the way I saw it we were going all the way to London and he wasn't going to come and see me. In the end, he felt so guilty that he agreed to come out but because he was nervous and anxious he drank half a litre of vodka before-hand and when he arrived he was a mess! So that night, the first time any of my housemates and the viewers had ever met him, he behaved like such a dick that everyone thought he was an idiot (when it was just because he was a bag of nerves!).

The minute he came through the door to the club, I could see how drunk he was. At one point he thought I'd walked off and left him in the club and he didn't understand a word I was saying so we had the biggest argument ever. Holly hated him, the others in the house hated him, and the viewers hated him. And Gary loved every minute.

This wasn't how I expected Mitch's first appearance on the show to be. That night, after we'd stopped filming, I went back to his house to see him. I still really loved him and I knew he wasn't that type of person at all. I felt partly to blame for forcing him to appear on telly.

Afterwards, everyone was having a go at me: 'Charlotte, you can't be with someone who's that nasty to you!' There was nothing I could do to persuade everyone it was just because he was drunk. I couldn't even start to think about the public not liking him because that would stress me out.

After that, and during the next series, he made my life a living hell. Being on camera had been everything he feared it would be, so now he was even more paranoid. He said I couldn't speak about him and he didn't like me being in there. He didn't want me to mention him on the show but how could I do that? When people asked about me and Mitch, what was I meant to say? 'Oh sorry, I'm not allowed to speak about him.' I couldn't do that and he knew it.

He just didn't want to be involved AT ALL.

Who the fuck did he think he was? Kanye West?

Mitchell had changed; he wasn't his old fun-loving self. It was ridiculous the way he was going on and it was putting too much pressure on me. Our relationship was starting to make me more unhappy than happy. I was trying so hard to make it work but it seemed like he didn't care. I started to ask myself, 'How can this relationship last when it seems to be only me that's fighting for it?'

He was pushing me away. I thought, 'I'm not wasting my time on someone who obviously doesn't care. It's my life, it's my job and now he's saying I can't even mention his name?' He wouldn't compromise and be part of the show. He was being a dickhead. I knew I had to give him an ultimatum and tell him all the things I was unhappy with.

This was all happening at the start of series nine, and I

left the house for a little bit to try and sort it out. I was on my way to my house when I sent him a text.

'I think we need to talk.'

'Right, OK, what time? I'm going out with the lads.'

'OK, well, if that's so important you can't even speak to me . . . then obviously this relationship means nothing.'

'Listen, Charlotte, I'll save you the hassle, I know exactly what you're going to say . . . let's just finish.'

I was shocked but I still had a few days out of the house before I had to go back to filming and he knew it, so I thought he'd contact me the next day, trying to sort it out. But he went out with his friends on the Friday, Saturday and Sunday and didn't bother to come and see me. Every second of it killed me, I was so upset, but I had to be strong. This wasn't a moment for Psycho Charlotte. I'd never been so calm with a boyfriend before. But I knew in myself that was what I had to do. I knew it was the end. It had to be. I couldn't keep going on like this – he didn't like me doing my job, which was part of my life. He wouldn't make any effort to make it even a little bit more stress-free.

I was due to go back into the house on the Monday night. That morning Mitch sent me a text: 'Come to my house.' He seemed to think he could send for me and it would all be fine. I don't know where I got the power from but I didn't reply. It was too late. I knew I had to be brave. I met the producers and handed my phone in.

As soon as I got back into the house and saw everyone

I got pissed out of my head and didn't stop for the rest of the series. I made sure I had the best time. I wasn't moping about any more; I was like a different person – I kissed other boys and I kissed Gary and I enjoyed myself.

And then the show was over again and as soon as I got out of the house the bubble burst. I had to face the reality that I wasn't with Mitch any more; that he wasn't going to be there for me when I came out. I really wanted to see him, I wanted to text him, and I wanted to look at his face. But I knew I couldn't. It was over.

I got back home to Newcastle and my brother Nathaniel said, 'You have ruined my life; Mitch is the best friend I ever had. How could you do this?' Nathaniel loved Mitch almost as much as I did. This was going to be hard . . .

THINGS GUARANTEED TO GET ME IN A MOOD

- **Me mam talking about my weight.** When I was bigger she would look at my belly. Once she sat me down with all the takeaway menus in the house and tried to give me 'the talk'. I said straight back to her, 'What's the problem? So what if I look like you when I'm older? You're fine with it!' I was so angry I just went to my friend's house and ordered a Chinese.

- **Mam and Dad using my car.** That fucks me off big style. I've got a new Range Rover, which I leave at home when I'm away. But I know they're always in it. I don't have my own house yet so my car is my treat. I like driving everywhere. I've got a fridge in there and a TV. So it's no wonder they always nick it.

- **When people fold paper and push the crease of it down really tightly.** It goes right through me.

- **When any of my friends who I've known for years call me 'babe', 'pet', 'flower' or 'mate'.** Sometimes Sophie will do it. Why call me 'babe'? My name is Charlotte. That's what you do when you don't remember people's names. I let Vicky get away with it because that's what she calls everyone.

- **When I hear about boys cheating on their girlfriends.**

- **When boys call girls slags.** They make out it's not OK for girls to sleep with a lot of boys yet it's fine the other way round? That makes me really angry.

- **Girls who wear high heels all the time.**

- **Girls who go to the gym in makeup and love pink.**

221

21

BELLY BLITZED AND BACK ON TRACK

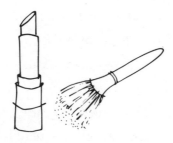

Someone said to me the other day, 'Did you put all that weight on just so you could do a fitness DVD?' But the truth is I'd just started to get fat from pure laziness. When I first entered the *Geordie Shore* house back in 2010, I was 8 stone 13 – that's my natural size – and growing up I've always been fairly skinny. But as the series progressed, so did my booze and food intake, and I never did any exercise. And then I got a boyfriend and we'd eat out all the time, which made it so much worse. I was over 11 stone by the time I decided to do anything about it.

The thing was, I was in complete denial. Even thought I'd put on weight, I'd dress to hide it. I'd always been clever and managed to cover my weight well. I forever wore baggy tops and leggings – things that only showed off the skinniest parts of my body, which were my arms and legs. I carried most of my weight and fat on my belly and I never let anyone see it.

And if *I* couldn't notice it, I'd just think no one else could, either. I honestly never thought I was getting big – no one ever told me. Everyone loved me for being 'the funny one' so no one seemed to notice my weight or pull me up on it because I was never known for my looks in the first place.

But there was one person who was guaranteed to say something. And that was me mam.

When I look back now, I was eating so much food it was actually disgusting. I'd have a takeaway nearly every night as well as eating a McDonald's during the day. I was getting bigger and bigger and it wasn't natural. It must have been hard for me mam to see her daughter letting herself go like that.

I took her to Dublin with me for a PA tour. That night I stayed out later than her and on the way back to the hotel I picked up a sneaky McDonald's. I'd already eaten loads of crap that day and Mam had made some remarks about it, which I hadn't liked. I crept back into the hotel so I wouldn't wake her up and because I was so scared about her seeing what I'd bought, I slumped in the dark just outside the bathroom door to eat it, hoping she was asleep and wouldn't notice. The room was pitch black but because I was mortal drunk I must have been making loads of noise. She got out of bed and all of a sudden, there she was in front of me, like the exorcist. I got the shock of my life.

'Charlotte, what are you doing?'

I was stuffing chips in my mouth.

'Oh, er, nothing, Mam.'

'What are you eating?'

'I just got a little McDonald's.'

'Why are you eating that? It's three o'clock in the morning!'

'I just got some chicken nuggets, that's all.'

Well, that was a lie. I had nuggets, yes, but I also had large fries, three dips and a double cheeseburger. I kept on eating it, hoping she couldn't see, but then she put the light on and grabbed it out of my hand.

'You need to stop this! I don't know what's wrong with you!' She was shouting at the top of her voice. 'All you do is drink and eat and it's getting so bad!'

I started screaming back at her. I was mortal and I was upset (not only was she saying I was fat but she was also pinching my food!). I grabbed the key to the room next door (we'd been given two rooms, we just chose to sleep together in one) and I ran as fast as I could down the corridor. We were making so much noise we must have woken everyone else up. I pushed her and she pushed me back. It was really bad. I eventually slept in the other room and the next day in the airport we didn't speak at all. It was the worst fight we'd ever had and it was heart-breaking. We were both crying. I never want that to happen again. It was horrible.

But it was a wake-up call.

Mams are always right. She always told me I was getting bigger and I never believed her. But now I look back at pictures and I was massive!

I'm one of those people who comfort eats. I'd go to my friends' houses and order a Chinese and I'd be crying to them that Mam was calling me fat while eating loads of egg fried rice!

Mam says she found it hard to tell me I had a problem and she didn't know how to tackle it because there's never a right way. Whichever way anyone puts it, it's never going to sound nice. But it needed to be said.

I love food. My favourite – as you've probably guessed – is a Chinese takeaway. If it never made you fat, here's what I'd order every day:

- Special fried rice
- A portion of chips and curry sauce – that's a northern thing
- Chicken chow mein
- Crispy Cantonese-style beef
- Duck and pancakes

I like to treat it like a buffet so you lay everything out, stuff yourself till you think you can't eat any more, then go back for seconds later. Is it any wonder I put on weight?

Another big weight wake-up was a photoshoot for *Nuts* magazine. It was just before I went into the *Big Brother* house – the team knew I was going in and wanted to have me on the cover for when the show started. I was used to doing stuff for *Nuts* when *Geordie Shore* first started, but this time round I'd got really big. I remember turning up to the shoot and all the clothes (well, knickers and bras) were sizes six and eight and when I put them on they were digging in so much that they were nearly cutting my skin. I was in the changing room trying to squeeze into them and I felt disgusting.

I locked the door and rang Mitch (we were still together at the time) and I was crying my eyes out. Mitch was really supportive about stuff like that and always made me feel so much better. Whereas some people might say, 'Stop being stupid,' he just said, 'Don't worry about it, I'm sure you'll look amazing and they won't put any pictures out where you look fat.' But I felt so insecure, I didn't want to stand in front of the camera feeling like that. My agent Kate knocked on the door and I snivelled, 'I will reimburse them for every penny they've spent on the shoot – just please tell me I don't have to do this.'

She said I didn't have to do anything that made me uncomfortable. But it was so late in the day I knew it would be hard for them to find a replacement and I didn't want to let anyone down.

Reluctantly, I went into the studio. I was crying in between takes. The photographer was really lovely but I would be glad never to see those pictures again in my life. I think I look humungous! They still put me on the cover but luckily I was inside the *Big Brother* house by then so I never had to see it on the newsstands.

After I came out of *Big Brother* I knew I needed to get fit, but the problem was, because I'd got so big I was embarrassed to even go to the gym. I was finding it so hard to get back into it. I started exercising but I wasn't really committing to anything. I'd start a bit then stop and I was still eating really badly.

Then I got my biggest wake-up call, the one that changed everything.

In June 2014, pap pictures of me in a red bikini came out which were taken when I was on holiday in Portugal. I was meant to have gone away with Mitch but we'd had a row so I went with my mate Lauren instead. By now I'd just come out of the *Geordie Shore* house after over a month of eating kebabs and pizzas and drinking every night. I'd put on even more weight. I knew I needed to do something about it but first I wanted a few days away from it all. Me and Lauren had a fab time drinking cocktails and just mucking about on the beach and on a pedalo as you do when you're on holiday with your mate. I never saw the photographer so I didn't even know he was taking pictures.

When I got back from Portugal the photos had gone *everywhere*. The headlines went on and on and I was on the cover of nearly every celebrity magazine.

'Charlotte Crosby flaunts curves in revealing red bikini.'

'What's happened to Charlotte Crosby?'

'Charlotte shows she's bigger and happier.'

But it was when I saw those photos that I had a real shock. I looked like I was wearing a fat suit! I've done some embarrassing things in my time but I can honestly say I haven't felt shame like that before. It's bad enough seeing a photo of yourself you don't like on a phone or on Facebook but you haven't felt true humiliation until you've experienced walking into a supermarket and seeing your rolls of fat on the front of a magazine. I remember seeing them and running outside and bursting into tears.

All I could think of was that hideous red bikini and when I saw it in *Heat* magazine I thought I looked really terrible. I joked to my friends that I looked like the Michelin woman. But inside I was so upset. I've still got a copy of that picture on my phone as a warning to myself.

I decided there and then that there were no more excuses. I had to sort myself out. Me mam was right. It was like a lightning bolt. There was nowhere to hide any more.

I've always been quite decisive and if I decide to do something, that's it, I do it. I asked my mates if they knew any fitness trainers and was introduced to a brilliant guy called Richard Callender. Richard had worked on ITV's *The Biggest Loser* so I thought, 'He's used to helping people even bigger than me!'

Richard and I hit it off straight away. I told him I hated exercise and found it boring. Basically I'd never done any in my life. So he came up with the idea of doing really short bursts of stuff so that I didn't get bored. Nothing longer than three minutes – perfect for my short attention span!

Richard was based in London which was great for when I was down in town for work, but it quickly became clear I'd also need some help when I was at home in Newcastle. I knew that Vicky Pattison had worked with David Souter, a trainer who was based not far from me in the north-east, so I got in touch with him for when I was at home. I needed both because I was always flitting between the two places.

We took it really slow at first; I just was training twice a week to try and improve my general fitness. I wasn't on a strict diet but I also wasn't eating McDonald's every day and I started noticing a difference straight away.

As I improved, my sessions went up to three to four times a week and I progressed from an hour to an hour and a half. I'd train in the mornings so I could fit it into my schedule, even when I was filming *Geordie Shore*. I didn't mind the getting up early but the actual exercise was so hard to begin with – there were times when I felt like giving the *whole thing* up. And other times when I was thinking, 'I literally cannot do this!'

I had so many moments when I wanted to eat a McDonald's or a Chinese. Every day I would crave something bad and would think, 'How can I possibly stick with this?' but over time I learnt that it was less about starving yourself of treats and more about knowing what to do afterwards. On the days when you slip up and cheat and eat something bad, it's the decision you make *afterwards* that counts. As long as you do something to correct it the next day, you're OK. You just have to get up the next morning, do a workout and you've almost cancelled it out. I still get it wrong and slip up and eat a sausage roll now and then but as long as I'm good the next day it doesn't matter. Slipping up is allowed as long as you don't carry on eating and eating and EATING!

Here's an example of my new diet:

Breakfast: eggs because they fill you up for longest, either scrambled, as an omelette or boiled (I used to skip breakfast and then around 11.30 a.m. I would have a massive McDonald's and still eat again at lunchtime!)

Snack: nuts, carrots and hummus or crackers with cottage cheese

Lunch: chicken salad

Dinner: steak (twice a week) or fish and vegetables or a stir-fry

I'm allowed a cheat day once a week and I'll nearly always have a McDonald's or a Chinese. McDonald's is the love of my life and giving it up was the hardest thing I've ever had to do.

As the weight started to come off, people kept asking me how I was doing it. And loads of my fans were saying stuff on Twitter like how inspired they were by the way I was losing all this weight. It was nice to know that people were noticing. Then Kate told me she'd had an email from a company asking if I'd be interested in doing a fitness DVD to show people how I'd lost the weight.

At first I wasn't sure. I thought it just seemed a bit presumptuous on my part to assume that people would want to buy a DVD with me sweating away in front of them! It's also quite a weird thing looking at yourself and admitting how overweight you were before you started training. Even though I didn't look like that any more, it was still the old me who was getting called 'fat' and over-weight, and I suppose the DVD offer made me confront how bad I'd let myself get.

There was also a part of me that thought I might let people down if I couldn't do it. But I'd seen my *Geordie Shore* castmate Vicky do a fitness DVD the year before and I remembered how she'd emerged at the end of the process looking amazing. So I thought, 'OK, maybe I'm wrong. Maybe I can do it? Maybe I should do it!'

I carried on training with Richard and David, doing the routines that would eventually become my DVD and eating a healthy diet. And slowly but surely I did it. I lost the weight! By the time we filmed the DVD I'd been training for six months and I'd lost over two and a half stone, drop-ping from a size sixteen to a size eight.

The DVD was called *Charlotte Crosby's 3-Minute Belly Blitz* and it was made up of three-minute, high-intensity workouts. We did the routines from the DVD every day in training and when I saw how my fitness levels were changing I felt so good. I hadn't just lost all the weight but I'd made my insides – my organs, my skin and everything – so much healthier.

Sometimes now I'll put videos on my Instagram of me doing my own DVD in front of the telly at home. My trainer David said to me the other day, 'It's so good that you show everyone you're doing because it looks really funny you doing it in your own living room.' I do it at least twice a week at home and I get the girls round. Me mam does it too, and me dad! But he looks ridiculous because he's so tall and gangly, trying to do all these girly skipping moves.

The DVD was released in January but I didn't dare let myself think it was going to be a success. People kept saying, 'It's going to be a best-seller,' but I would reply, 'Let's not get our hopes up.'

When it came out it went to number one in the fitness chart just on pre-orders. This sounded impressive until I found out that pretty much all fitness DVDs do that – if you have a decent amount of followers on Twitter then it's easy to get the pre-orders in, so it doesn't mean much.

It was only when it went to number one in the retail charts that I really knew it was a big deal. It started flying off the shelves and I couldn't register it in my head. It didn't feel real. Being number one in the retail charts means it's selling more than all the other DVDs in all the shops. Suddenly *Charlotte Crosby's 3-Minute Belly Blitz* was selling more than *Frozen* and *Downton Abbey*! And that's when I finally realised, 'Whoa, this is huge.' The fitness DVD company were really pleased and I was secretly chuffed to know that Vicky's DVD hadn't made it anywhere near number one in the retail chart!

Wow. What the hell was going on?

I went into HMV with Melissa and saw it on the shelves – that's when it really hit me. I looked at it and said to her, 'Should I buy it? I'm a bit embarrassed. Do you think anyone will notice it's me buying my own DVD?' She smiled, 'No, I don't think they will, don't worry.' So we took it to the front counter, I put it down and the man looked at the front cover, looked up at me and said knowingly, 'Is this yours?'

I grinned and whispered, 'Yeah!'

The next thing I knew I was being told it was the fastest-selling fitness DVD of *all time*! I'd beaten everyone in the entire fitness market – including Davina McCall who is the queen of fitness. I felt like a pop star.

It obviously helped sales that I did loads of press to promote it. We travelled up and down the country to sign-ings and personal appearances. I was on Radio 1, *The Wright Stuff* and *Mail* Online every day for eleven days. Everywhere I went I carried a giant cardboard cut-out of me when I was fat, wearing the red bikini. It was the same height as me so you could see exactly how I looked before and after the weight loss. I nicknamed her 'Big Charlotte' and people would stop me and ask for a selfie with me and Big Charlotte. My agent even joked that she might sign her up because she was better behaved than me! By the time I got to the end of the week of press interviews, Big Charlotte had been decapitated, but I still dragged her round with me – head or no head.

My DVD cover was even projected onto the Houses of Parliament! When someone told me it was going to happen I thought it was a joke – the next thing I knew it was all over the *Mail* Online. My bum was in one of the windows. I was literally mooning David Cameron in his office!

After my DVD came out, I found some old footage of me taken by Richard when I first started training and posted it on Twitter. It was amazing to see how much I'd changed. Richard had filmed me doing lunges on his camera phone during one of my first sessions and I was so unfit! It was the first bit of exercise I'd done in years; I'd completely given up and didn't see the point because I never lost any weight (er, might have had something to do with the fact I was eating so many Chinese takeaways . . .). So when you watch this 'before' clip I'm in these tiny yellow shorts and my belly is hanging over the top of them – it literally wobbles when I do a lunge. Now I look at it I think it looks like an elephant walking along a tightrope.

CHARLOTTE'S WORDS OF WISDOM ON: BODIES

I have battled with my weight over the years and made so many mistakes in the way I used to think – for example, believing you only look good if you have a booty like Beyoncé, legs like Kate Moss and a chest like Katie Price (well, her old one anyway).

Then I realised you need to stop trying to be like other people and just try to be the best person that YOU can possibly be.

Everyone has favourite parts of their bodies and parts that they maybe don't like as much. I LOVE my legs and arms but I always struggle with my belly; it's the last place the weight comes off and the first place it goes on! I'm sure you will have one part of your body you struggle with too, it just means you have to work a little harder on that part – but believe me, it will be worth it in the end.

22

DÉJÀ VU

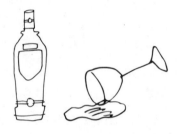

The more weight I lost, the more confident I felt and I was quickly getting back to my old self again.

Mitch and I had been finished for a few months now and I got offered the chance to be in MTV's *Ex on the Beach*, a reality show where eight single people looking for love get stuck on a beach with their exes. I thought, 'I'm single, it's a job opportunity – something I can write about in my memory book!' I was sent in as Gary's ex – he was already on the show – and by the time I got there he was getting close to a girl called Anita. Despite the fact that

Gary and me had been getting it on again in series nine of *Geordie Shore*, I knew that it had just been a show thing. And when I saw him on *Ex on the Beach* it just confirmed everything I'd ever thought about him – that he used me. Because when we were on *Ex on the Beach* he didn't want anything to do with me; there were far better girls in there for him so he didn't need me for his airtime.

He did authentically seem to like Anita though and was so lovey dovey – he was touching her at every opportunity, kissing her forehead and stroking her legs. It was the first time I'd ever seen him behave like that with a girl (he was *never* like that with me). It was so odd watching him get all soppy because I didn't know he had the capacity to be like that. I didn't have any feelings for him, though – deep down in the back of my heart I was still pining for Mitch.

After *Ex on the Beach* we filmed series ten of *Geordie Shore* and it was during this series that it was revealed that Gary has a SERIOUS GIRLFRIEND.

I suspect Gary had been dating Lillie on the quiet for longer than he let on. But it was only in series ten that he went public. I got quite emotional when I went to meet her on the show and it must've looked like I was still in love with Gary – but it was more that the whole thing had been made into such a big deal, everyone was asking me how I felt that Gary had finally settled down, the cameras were on me all the time and it was just dead intense. I was also thinking about Mitch – seeing Gary with Lillie made me realise I'd thrown away someone I genuinely loved and cared for.

I do like Lillie, though – she's gorgeous, skinny, pretty and dead nice. She's the perfect lady so Gary is lucky to have her.

All throughout series ten I wanted to get back with Mitch. I wasn't interested in getting it on with anyone else. I was ready to make another go of it.

We'd been texting and talking again and he said he wanted to meet up. So I asked him to come and visit me one day when I was a guest on *Celebrity Juice*.

I'll never forget his expression when I saw him again for the first time. He hadn't seen me since I'd lost all the weight and I wish I could've videoed his face when I walked up to him. I went to meet him in his hotel before filming began and as I walked along the corridor towards him, his jaw dropped and his mouth fell wide open. He gasped, 'I can't believe it, Charlotte! You look amazing!' Then he poked the bones that were jutting out of my dress and said, 'You almost look *too* thin.' I grinned at him, 'You'll get used to it, Mitchell.' I felt sexy and I knew then he wanted to get back with me. We spent the night together after the show and immediately I felt all the old feelings coming back again. But although it was nice and I still loved him, I couldn't stop thinking about the fact that we'd both been with other people since we'd been apart. I couldn't get it out of my head and it killed me every time I looked at him. I didn't see someone who was my boyfriend, I saw someone I'd lost and who'd slept with other girls – and I never want to go back to that stage ever *ever* again.

Ever since we've been back together, it's like I'm with a whole different person. This isn't the same Mitch he was before we finished – he's finally back to his old self, the one he was at the start when I first met him at the PA in Reading. It used to be me saying I wanted us to move in together and buy a house whereas he just wanted to be with his friends. But he's changed now. All he wants is to settle down and spend as much time together as possible. I got a tattoo of his initials for Valentine's Day and he kisses it at night. He's got so soppy. I think being apart from each other made us realise what we'd both lost and we appreciate each other so much more now. Mitch doesn't moan about my work or me being away from him when I go into *Geordie Shore*; we trust each other and it feels like we're together forever. Everything finally feels right.

We even got engaged! Well, so everyone thought, anyway. Mitch had come away with me to Australia for another work trip and one night we got absolutely mortal at a PA. I passed out on the bed as soon as we got back to the hotel and when I woke up in the morning Mitch turned to me with a worried look on his face.

'Look on your Twitter. I think I've done something bad.'

I looked on my Twitter and he'd taken a semi-naked pic of me slumped on the bed. I said, 'I look quite good. Actually I look wicked! I'm buzzing. I'm going to put it in my Instagram!'

He was still worried. 'It's not that . . .' he said. 'Keep scrolling down.'

Then I saw the tweet. It had been sent from my account so it looked like it had come from me.

'OH MY GOD I SAID YES!' it read, followed by an emoji of a wedding ring.

Mitch – what have you done?!

Then I saw that it had had 18,000 retweets.

Shit.

And there were loads of messages of congratulations.

Double shit.

Sam Faiers had tweeted congratulations, so had Luisa Zissman, and I think Chanelle Hayes had sent me one too. And obviously there were loads from my followers. There was also a message from an Australian radio show wanting to do the first exclusive interview . . .

How was I going to tell everyone this wasn't real?

Obviously everyone I was close to back home knew it wasn't true. Me mam and Melissa spoke on the phone and laughed about it – they knew I'd have said something to them first. And Dad would've killed Mitch if he hadn't asked his permission!

To begin with I just found the whole thing really funny but after a while it dawned on me that if Mitch was ever to propose properly then no one would believe us! Afterwards Mitch started talking about how he'd planned exactly what was going to happen when he did do it for real. He kept saying, 'It's going to be so romantic . . .'

Maybe he was just testing things all along. Perhaps he wanted to know what my reaction would be? I still don't know why he really did it, I think he was just mortal and thought it was funny.

It's all so brilliant between us now and I still get butter-flies in my belly whenever I'm on my way to meet him. I went on holiday to Cape Verde with the girls recently and I couldn't wait to see him when I got back. I was so excited driving down to London that I had to keep ringing him to tell him to hurry up and finish work. When I got there we cuddled and kissed for ages and we had sex. Then he had to do a load of estimates for work – he's got a painting and decorating business – so I sat next to him and watched a documentary about giant blue whales on YouTube. That's the kind of thing we do.

We have such a laugh together and can talk about anything and everything. Today I got back from the gym and we lay in bed for an hour and talked about how much our legs were aching. He's just started back training too and we ended up having a competition about how much pain we were in and it got into a bit of a war about whose legs were hurting more!

And you know every couple has weird voices that they do? Well, mine and Mitch's aren't even voices, they're just strange noises that sound like aliens. It's like we're not even saying anything – just slurring like we're drunk. We have stupid names for each other, too. I call him anything begin-ning with B – like Bob or Bab or Bombala. And he likes to give me names after different objects. So he'll say, 'How's my little light bulb today?' Or 'How's my satchel doing?' Or 'You are a little flannel!'

Isn't it weird how couples do that? Then you forget when you're out in public and people give you funny looks. We do it in front of our mams and dads all the time and they just roll their eyes.

We fart in front of each other all the time, too. Mitch and me are very open about stuff like that. That's why I love him – we're like two best friends.

And he doesn't even mind if I have a hairy vagina. I wax it sometimes when it's his birthday or a special occasion but he's perfectly happy with a hairy fairy too. It's a good job because I don't really like waxing. The first time I got a full vagina wax was in Australia. It was an all over one and I had to put my legs behind my head to get to my bum hole.

Mitch doesn't mind that I'm not very hygienic either. I had a shower this morning but it's been a good three days since I had one before that. I get home after a long day and I haven't got time, I'm tired. Oh, and I snore! Gary used to moan about it all the time but Mitch hardly mentions it. Now that's love.

23

CHARLOTTE FOR PM

As part of the promotion for series ten of *Geordie Shore* we pretended we were running in the election as the *Geordie Shore* Party Party. I had a megaphone and was shouting stupid stuff about the laws we'd make if we were in government.

Imagine if I did get to run the country? I reckon I'd make it a much more fun place. Here's what I'd do if I could make the laws:

1. Give spray tans on the NHS. You can go as dark as you want, it's totally up to you. But I'd recommend mahogany.

2. The Houses of Parliament would be turned into a massive superclub. It'd be quite expensive entry just because of where it is but the drinks would be dead cheap and the music would be good. The PM's office would be the VIP area and all the MPs, including David Cameron, would have to learn to do the slut-drop dance move (he's quite tall and athletic so I think he'd be good at it).

3. We'd get rid of all public transport and we'd use jetpacks.

4. We'd only let the hottest people into the country. So that's people like Leonardo DiCaprio, Channing Tatum, David Beckham and the Victoria's Secret models.

5. I would ban guns, knives, violence, murder and beetroot (it dyes your fingers and all your clothes and it tastes disgusting).

6. I'd banish all of *Made in Chelsea* and *TOWIE* and I'd live in a green castle in Hyde Park.

It wouldn't be the first time a person from *Geordie Shore* has dabbled in politics either. Vicky and I had a long conversation (well, argument) about Emily Pankhurst in one of our earlier episodes (she's actually called Emmeline but I like Emily). I was telling the girls that I thought if Emily Pankhurst was alive today she'd be so angry about the fact that boys walk around thinking that it's cool to sleep with loads of women but girls can't do the same – whenever a girl sleeps with loads of boys she gets called a 'slag'. But Vicky wasn't having any of it. 'That is *not* what Emily Pankhurst stood for at all!' she said. I argued, 'Well, if Emily Pankhurst was alive today, I think she *would* be annoyed that there are still different rules for men and women over something as natural as shagging and she would fling herself under a horse to save anyone from being called a slag!' (I've since found out apparently it wasn't even Emily Pankhurst who did the horse thing . . . it was someone called Emily Davison. They had a lot of Emilys in those days.) Anyway, Vicky was having none of it. 'No it's not. It's disgusting! This is a shambles. Emily Pankhurst would be embarrassed by you!' But I thought what I was saying made perfect sense. As far as I was concerned, that's what modern-day feminism is all about. After all, feminism is about equality, isn't it?

I'm not sure I'd have much time to go into politics and run the country, if I'm honest. My fitness DVD hasn't been the only thing keeping me busy. Just after *Big Brother* I was approached about doing my own clothing range. It was two guys called Jamie and Adam from a company called InTheStyle and they told me I could design my own range, have complete control and be involved in everything right down to the last stitch.

I had my own clothing range in series two of *Geordie Shore* but we just went to wholesalers and picked out stuff I liked and I put my name on it. But I wanted to do my own designs and feel like they were my own. What is the point of saying something is yours if you've had hardly anything to do with it?

When that ended, I met Jamie and Adam and I knew straightaway they were the sort of people I wanted to work with. Everything they suggested I agreed with and I thought, 'This is exactly what I want to do!'

The whole process was amazing and it just felt right. I'd go to meetings with them feeling like I was dead important and professional. They wanted me to get all my ideas together and pull out favourite styles from my wardrobe so I'd come home and sit with an A3 folder making mood boards of different things I liked. I had a denim mood board, a white one, a skirt mood board . . . I was cutting up magazines for hours. I was so busy but I loved every second of it.

Then they asked me to do another mood board to come up with a name for my brand. I did a spider diagram of all my favourite words:

WANDERLUST
means 'the want to travel!' One day I wish to travel the world with just a backpack and the people I love will be all riding unicorns.

NOSTALGIA
I've always loved this word and it was the one I picked for my clothing range. It means recalling a memory, which makes you feel happy.

UNICORN
unicorn isn't just an amazing word it's an amazing magical being which 100 percent exists somewhere.

CHARLOTTE'S WEB OF WORDS

NA
my favourite of all words just means 'no' but I usually like to shout it loudly about everything!

ORIFICE
I like it when the dictionary over complicates words. For example this one just means hole! Hahahaha! I suppose it's a nicer way to talk about your bum-hole: 'Bum orruphus.'

So I settled on Nostalgia and that became the name for my clothing (I think I also had 'Fun' as an option at one point but that just sounded crap).

Next, Jamie and Adam took my mood boards to their designers who did sketches in 'collections' so I could see which ones I liked and which I didn't. Then we had to choose the fabric; I looked through over 500 fabrics and it took about two hours! It was brilliant, though, I felt like Gucci or Dolce and Gabbana. It took six months in total before we had clothes on the shelves. And just like my fitness DVD, it started to do really well and I was dead chuffed. I love Jamie and Adam, too. We've grown so close now, it's not like we're work colleagues, we're like best friends. They're partners in real life as well as work – Adam is the serious business head and Jamie is the manager. Together they work so well. If they ever split up I think I'd cry.

Nostalgia wasn't just a success in the UK; it did really well in Australia, too. This meant that when I visited Oz I could combine doing press for MTV, my fitness DVD, PAs *and* my clothing range. But the problem with having so many things to promote is that sometimes you can push yourself too far – which means burnout and bad moods!

I spent five weeks in Australia this year on a massive tour and at one point we did four different destinations in twenty-eight hours and I didn't even see a bed! We travelled from Perth to Darwin, Darwin to Adelaide,

Adelaide to the Gold Coast, Gold Coast to Brisbane and Brisbane to Sydney!

No hotel room, no bed, no sleep.

It didn't help that I got mortal drunk and started stressing out on the plane. The poor air hostess didn't know what to do but I just couldn't take any more and it had all got on top of me – I was tired, drunk and my eyes were burning from lack of sleep. I knew I had to get straight off the plane and go to a festival for an appearance, then I had to get another flight straight to a nightclub for a PA . . . I was getting so stressed about it. I know it sounds over the top but I felt a bit like I was having a nervous breakdown.

I try not to get moody because I know how lucky I am, but there are times when stuff gets to me. And because I have to do so many interviews – sometimes in a row – I need to get it all out of my system beforehand so I don't let it affect my job. So I've developed what I call my 'negative time', which I channel before an interview to get rid of any moodiness!

One particular moody moment was when I was in New Zealand; I'd just finished a manic week where I was working morning to night and I was so happy because I thought I had the day off to chill and go to the gym. I woke up that morning to a knock on the door. It was someone from MTV New Zealand. They were here to take me to a series of press interviews for *Geordie Shore*.

I couldn't help myself. I was so angry. The man from

MTV was called Ben and I greeted him with such a horrible negative manner he must've instantly hated me.

'Ben! I'm so pissed off!' I shouted at him as he walked through the door. 'I thought I had a day to myself!'

The poor boy didn't know what had hit him. 'I don't know what to do, Charlotte. I really want this to be a positive day. You have lots of interviews lined up and I want them to be fun.'

He was so worried I was going to be in a bad mood with the press. But what he didn't know is that I would never do that; no matter what has happened to me to get me in a huff there's no way I'd ever let my bad mood show – I just need to have my time to be negative beforehand. That way I can get it all out of my system and let the positivity break through!

'Let's just be positive, Charlotte!' By now, Ben was pleading with me.

But I wasn't having it. 'No, Ben, why don't you just be negative with me for a bit? Just for an hour – I'm sick of being positive.'

'But I'm scared you'll be in a bad mood when I take you to do the interviews,' he reasoned.

'I promise I won't.'

It was like we were having a standoff and we hated each other at first. But slowly but surely I knocked down his positive mental attitude and gradually we started to grow a bond.

The problem was, I was so busy telling him to be negative that I sent him into a mad spin. And as we drove in the car on the way to the interviews, he started telling me that he didn't know when his next pay cheque was coming in, that he wasn't happy in his life, then he started saying things like, 'There's a fruit fly that has flown into New Zealand which means we can't take fruit out of our homes in case the other food gets infected. AND I CAN'T EVEN EAT A BANANA!'

Shit, what had I done? He was properly going nuts now. 'OK, Ben,' I said calmly, 'I need to be positive now! I'm negatived out!' I needed to snap him out of it. I started trying to talk about loads of positive things: 'What a great day! You'll be eating bananas in no time!' I tried everything to get him happy again and just before we arrived at my first TV interview he was back to normal. Thank fuck for that!

I did my interview and I was really happy and upbeat and Ben could breathe a sigh of relief that I'd been able to turn my bad mood around.

All in all, New Zealand was an amazing experience. I did a PA there and I felt like I was P Diddy – there were so many people in the club and they were all chanting my name! At one point they carried me across their heads in a rubber dingy because I said I'd always wanted to do it (well, ever since I saw that rich guy called Dan Bilzerian whatshisname doing it on Instagram anyway).

I got so carried away with it all that I got one of my boobs out on stage and kissed two girls. I was mortal and

I would have done anything – the crowd was going nuts and I was going more nuts.

Nights like that are real pinch-yourself moments. To see all those people that excited to see *me* just feels so surreal and it really takes my breath away.

That trip to Australia and New Zealand was filled with such highs and real lows, too. It was while I was out there that I heard the terrible news that Carol McGiffin had breast cancer.

I was with Jamie and Adam from the clothing range; we were in a hotel in Australia and woke up really hungover after a big night out. Jamie was looking at the Internet and suddenly said, 'Oh, Charlotte! You never told us Carol had cancer.'

I was floored.

'What?'

'It's on the *Daily Mail* today and in all the magazines and on the news.'

'Show me.'

I didn't quite believe it. My head was pounding anyway from last night's booze and slowly the words came into focus. I started reading the reports and my eyes welled up with tears. The front-page picture on one of the papers was of Carol with a bald head; I stared at it blankly and felt goose pimples all over my body.

What the fuck? Why hadn't she told me? It all suddenly started to make sense. Looking back I should have known something was wrong. I'd invited her to events like the launch party for my clothing range and she'd always say no and that she was too busy or made some excuse that she was going away or something. I hadn't seen her for about nine months because she kept dodging meeting up. Now it made sense why I hadn't seen her in so long and why she hadn't come to any of my things. She'd been going through this massive, horrible, hideous thing in her life. I felt awful, I was so close to her, she'd become one of my good friends and I just couldn't believe this was happening to someone I cared about.

I sent her a text straight away.

We have this in-joke where I always say she's going to 'Thailand' whenever she's going somewhere – I get the places confused all the time and she shouts at me. We also talk about this guy called 'Big Al' when really he's called Jeff. I just get everything wrong and it winds her up.

'You idiot!' I texted, 'You had me thinking you were going to Thailand with Big Al for the last twelve months when really that wasn't the case – why didn't you tell me?'

She texted back straight away,

'Oh little'un, you do make me laugh, you've still got it. I didn't want to tell you and bring you down or put a dampener on all the good things going on in your life.'

I texted back another silly message. I didn't want her thinking I was feeling sorry for her because she must have had that all the time.

She replied laughing. She said, 'Let's meet up – your text

has been the first one to make me laugh in a long time, I want you to tell me all your funny stories.'

We've tried to meet up since I got back but it still hasn't happened yet. The last time we'd arranged to go for lunch but she was feeling too ill and had to cancel so I told her it was more important for her to get a rest. I love Carol so much and I know she'd hate anyone pitying her so I can't wait to meet up and have a good laugh and a drink.

24

F*CK ME I'M FAMOUS

It's a weird thing – people knowing who you are.

If someone had sat me down after that disastrous PA in Cambridge when everyone was shouting 'Who are ya? Who are ya?' and told me I'd have people in Australia running up begging for autographs like I'm Lady Gaga or something, I'd have told them to do one.

But at some PAs now I feel like I'm the most famous person on the planet. James and I used to have a special patter that we gave whenever we were on stage. I'd have the microphone first and I'd say, 'Hello (insert whichever city you're in)!'

259

Then I'd pass it to James and he'd shout, 'How ya fucking doin'?'

Then the mic would come back to me and I'd say, 'Who's getting mortal tonight?!' and the crowd would go crazy because obviously that's such a *Geordie Shore* word.

James would then shout, 'Let's get the music back on and let's get dancing!' and then we'd dance on the stage and think we were Beyoncé and Jay Z. We'd be bending down touching people's hands, getting selfies with people, kissing them on the cheek . . .

I remember one time this boy came up to me and got me to do my signature on his arm and the next night he came back to another PA and showed me his arm and he'd had my signature tattooed onto it! I said to him, 'Why did you do that?' Not only was it crazy but also he had been about the 700th person who I'd signed for and I'd just scribbled it! I hadn't even done it properly! If I'd known he wanted it on him for life I'd have made it much neater. I don't even think it looked like my real signature . . . I didn't dare tell him that, though.

It is mad people knowing who you are but it can affect the people you're with more than you. Mitch and I went to Thorpe Park once, but we forgot it was half term. It was rammed and every single child was running after me asking for a selfie! In the end I had to go to the gift shop and buy a disguise. I came out in a Thorpe Park hat and sunglasses with a scarf wrapped round my neck. It got to the point that Mitch got really annoyed because he's always the one who gets asked to take the photo and he started walking away. I was shouting, 'Stop walking away because then I can't find you and I'm wandering around like a tit!' Then we had a massive argument in the middle of Thorpe Park.

Sometimes I'm not quite so brave about those situations, though. I can get quite bad anxiety sometimes, especially with men. If I ever walk into a situation where there's a big group of blokes, there will always be one who will try to act like the lad and someone will start shouting, 'You Geordie slag.' It can be horribly intimidating and it makes me anxious.

As I said earlier, though, one of the *best* parts of being on TV is getting to meet other people on TV. It always seems really strange when I see famous people and they know who I am. Like at the National Television Awards when Jonathan Ross was screaming at me, 'Charlotte! Charlotte!' Now *that* was crazy.

I was walking into the after-party when I heard my name but I didn't know who was calling me to start with. When I turned round it was Jonathan standing there, smiling at me. What was going on? When people like that speak to me I get so star-struck I don't know how to act (I wonder if there are classes you can go to that teach you how to deal with famous people?).

'Hi, Jonathan, how's it going?'

'How are you? I'm sick of the bloody sight of you every-where! Well done on your *3-Minute Belly Blitz*!'

What the hell? This is so weird.

Then my agent Kate came over and started asking when

he would be having me on his show! 'I'd love to have her on the show!' he said. But I doubt in any way, shape or form I would ever go on *The Jonathan Ross Show*. There's no way I'd be allowed to sit on the same sofa as the likes of Justin Timberlake and Lady Gaga.

He was so down to earth, though, what a lovely man.

That night at the National Television Awards was mental from start to finish. *Geordie Shore* was up for an award: Best Multi-channel Programme. We were up against *Celebrity Juice*, *Game of Thrones* and something else I can't remember. We were convinced we were going to win. The whole cast had been campaigning for three weeks on Twitter and Facebook – we thought we had it in the bag. Between all of us we had about five million followers!

But first I had to get my outfit. I'd been searching for inspiration on Instagram and started following this designer called MT Costello. I found him on Cheryl Cole's feed because she wore this gorgeous dress to some event and he'd designed it. At first I thought, 'Is it too much of a long shot to think I can get a dress from the man who lets Cheryl wear his clothes?' but then I thought, 'You know what? I'm going to try it!' So I looked on the website and saw this stunning red gown but it was from the new collection so I couldn't order it online so I decided I'd get Kate on the case. She emailed their office to explain about the event and told them who I was and that our show was up for an award and asked if there was any chance of getting hold of the dress I'd seen. The reply came back and the man (the

M stood for Michael) was dead nice and said he should have one in that week and would be able to sort it out!

It got to five days before the event and there I was, thinking I was Billy Big Balls because I had a dress by an amazing designer who designs stuff for Cheryl Cole and 'my dress is going to be the best and everyone's going to be so jealous!' when all of a sudden I get an email off Kate . . .

'We've got a bit of bad news on the dress front. Michael Costello has been back in touch and he's done some research on you and he's found out that you've said some bad things about Kim Kardashian in the past. And because he works really closely with Kim and all the family he's really sorry but he can't now send you the dress.'

What the actual fuck?

What the hell had I said about her?

Then I remembered. I had been on *This Morning* and I was on a section called 'Rate or Slate' and a picture of Kim Kardashian had come up as one of the images to discuss. Kim was wearing this white tracksuit thing and it was massive around her arse, so when the camera came to me I said, 'I'm definitely slating this! I don't know why she'd wear something like this! All it does is look like she's got a gigantic nappy on and looks like she's shit herself.'

I was so angry with myself now for saying it but how could I have known what would happen?

I later found out that MT Costello dresses the Kardashians for nearly *everything* – I looked on all their Instagrams and nearly every dress they wore was by him! They obviously love his stuff and wear it all the time so there's no way he'd want to piss them off.

But this left me with four days to find a dress. I was in a right panic but then I found an amazing shop in North London called Dress to Party and I found this beautiful navy gown that was dead classy. In the magazines afterwards people wrote, 'Charlotte looked completely different!' So I reckon it was meant to happen in the end because I got on the 'Best Dressed' list in four different places! I felt amazing; I went for a totally different look to usual and pinned all my hair back – it wasn't down and big like it normally is – and I had dramatic eyes and a darker lip. When I looked in the mirror I thought 'Whoa!' I looked like someone from *Downton Abbey*. It was a nice change.

Celebrity Juice beat us to the NTA. I was gutted.

Kris Jenner was on the stage presenting the award and when it was announced I was fuming! When the cameras went on us we were supposed to pull a happy face but I was screaming 'Noooo!' and everyone was telling me to calm down.

Afterwards I saw Keith Lemon and the guys from *Celebrity Juice* in the corridor when I was walking to the toilet and I said, 'You idiots!' Keith replied, 'Well, sorry, Charlotte, but we were always going to win, we are the better show!' and everyone laughed. I've been on *Celebrity Juice* so much now that I know all the producers and one of them said, 'Can't you just think you won with us?' and I said, 'No! It's nothing like that!'

It didn't help that when Kris Jenner was on stage she said our name wrong! She called us *Gordie Shore*! She messed it up completely and because she spoke too fast our image didn't even get played on the screen. And she was wearing a ridiculous fur coat that made her look like a giant ostrich. I think there's something spookily weird going on with me and the Kardashians; we're literally always clashing. There are strange forces at work!

The NTAs are so crazy. There are all these celebrities in a huge room but it gets really messy. When you see it on telly and the cameras are on a certain group of people sitting down, what you don't see is that off-camera around them, it's anarchy! The celebs are all getting out of their seats, talking to people or wandering off to go to the loo or smoke cigarettes. When they disappear there are random people on stand-by who have been paid to be 'seat fillers' – so if a camera is about to focus on a certain place and there's no one in their seat then the seat fillers swoop in. I guess you can never control what celebs do!

The cast of *Coronation Street* were sat opposite us and they did the sad speech about Anne Kirkbride who played Deirdre Barlow. It was weird seeing them all so close, they were all really down and sobbing in their seats. It was heart-breaking having to watch them getting so upset; that's when you realise how close they are.

Dermot O'Leary was hosting it and when he walked down the aisle he grabbed me and said, 'Well done on your *3-Minute Belly Blitz*, Charlotte!'

Mad, huh?

The next time I met one of my celeb idols was when I started being a regular on *This Morning* and I was on the show with Peter Andre. Peter and Jordan were the celebrities I grew up watching on TV, I loved their shows when I was younger so I got really shy and nervous when I met him. But he was lovely and said, 'Would you meet my assistant? She loves your show, she wants a picture with you.'

How cool was that?!

But the time I was *massively* in awe of someone, so much so that I couldn't even speak and was lost for words and stuttering, was when I was a guest on *Britain's Got More Talent*. Ant and Dec were rehearsing for the live show and I was stood at the top of the stairs and they were at the bottom. I was waiting for my cue to go on when all of a sudden I felt a tap on my back. Ant had walked all the way from the stage, up four flights of stairs *just to come and say hello to me*. How the fuck did he even know who I was? He tapped me on the back and I turned round and there was Ant with his massive forehead standing there right in front of me! I froze; I didn't know what to say. I felt like I was having to catch my breath when he said, 'Hi, Charlotte, how you doing?'

I couldn't even register that he knew my name!

'Hi, Ant, I'm great, thank you. How are ya?'

'It's so great to have you down finally. Are you enjoying everything? Are you looking forward to the live show?'

'I'm so excited, Ant, thank you so much. I love the show, I watch it all the time!'

'Well, that's great – and you're doing great for yourself now, aren't you, eh?'

I didn't know what to say. I went silent.

'Don't look so shocked,' he laughed. 'It's a good thing.'

'Yeah . . .'

'Well, well done on *Big Brother* and everything. I just came to say hi. I've got to run back downstairs anyway.' By now people were shouting his name. 'Ant! We need you back down here!'

I had to get my phone! I ran to my dressing room, grabbed my phone and immediately rang Mam. We watched *Saturday Night Takeaway* all the time when I was growing up. Every weekend we'd be there with our takeaway and popcorn – me mam *loves* Ant and Dec. And now I'd just met one of them! Me mam was screaming down the phone, 'I can't believe it! I *knew* they'd be lovely in real life!'

After the show, Ant said, 'Charlotte, come and speak to our PA – we want to book you for when we do *Saturday Night Takeaway Live*,' and I replied, 'Tell me the dates and I'm there!' In the end I did all three nights in Newcastle and on one of them I did 'I'm a Celebrity Get Out of Me Ear' where they were both talking to me through an earpiece telling me what to do. I had to go into the back room where someone was serving drinks and they told me I had to ask for a drink and then ask someone if they were pregnant! They were making me do really stupid, funny things and at one point I had to speak in a really posh voice.

Another 'starry moment' was when I was on *The Xtra Factor*. I was on a panel with Boyd Hilton from *Heat* magazine and Katie Hopkins. After it aired I got a Twitter message from David Walliams.

'Hi Charlotte' – this was so random because I'm a massive fan of David Walliams; I think he's hilarious and I've been following him on Twitter for ages – 'I just wanted to say you were great on tonight's *Xtra Factor*, I tuned in because my friend Boyd was also on the panel and he said you were really down to earth and lovely, well done.'

I wrote back, 'Oh my God, thank you so much! I watch *BGT* all the time and I literally think you make the show.'

What?! This was another time I thought, 'What the hell is going on with my life? What's happening to me?'

I also did *The Xtra Factor* on the year Sam Bailey won. I was on the final show, which meant that all the judges were on it too. I was in the corridor waiting to go into the studio in Wembley, it was a dead tight corridor, and so the judges had no choice but to walk past us. I was with Rylan, Leigh Francis and Nicholas McDonald – the young boy who was in Louis' group. One by one the judges came by. Nicole Scherzinger floated past looking beautiful, I've never been so mesmerised by someone in my entire life. She and Rylan spoke because that was the year that he was in her group. Gary Barlow walked out and said 'hi' to everyone and then Sharon Osbourne came past and was having a laugh with

Nicholas, saying, 'I'm getting you pissed tonight!' (even though he was under age) and Nicholas was laughing his head off. Then Louis Walsh walked out and said 'hi' to Rylan and Leigh before looking at me. 'Who are you?' he asked. 'I'm Charlotte,' I said at which he replied, 'Oh! Are you the girl from *Geordie Shore?*' I smiled back, 'Yeah that's me!' Then Louis turned back to Nicholas and said something about him having a shag sorted that night!

I literally didn't know where to put myself. I was so angry and embarrassed. I felt like a piece of shit. Afterwards I kept thinking of all these things I could have said back to him. You know when you think of clever retorts but it's too late? I so wish I'd said, 'Why, Louis? Are *you* going to shag him?'

That comment really hurt me.

25

THE FUTURE'S BRIGHT, THE FUTURE'S MAHOGANY

So much has changed since I first walked through the doors of the *Geordie Shore* house and necked a Jägerbomb with Vicky.

At the start of series ten, I sat looking round the table at all the housemates. By now we had even more new people join us: Sophie's cousin Marnie came in series seven, and we also had Aaron, Kyle, Chloe and Nathan. As we all did a 'cheers' to mark the start of the show, I got a flashback to when we did that for the first time when we started in 2010. And it just wasn't the same. The only originals left were me, Gary and Holly . . . and I got a bit sad.

I do have a lot of time for the new housemates, though – and Kyle was someone I'd met *way before* he even entered *Geordie Shore*. I actually dated him for a few months! He was a mate of Sophie's and she introduced us when we were in town during the break after series one. We didn't have anything serious or call each other boyfriend and girl-friend (we *definitely* never went out for meals) but it was very weird when I saw him come into the house in series eight. I was dating Mitch at the time and he was paranoid enough about Gary – so when I saw my ex-boyfriend come in I thought, 'As if I need another reason for Mitch to kick off!' I remember running into the boys' bedroom, crying my eyes out really dramatically and covering all the cameras with T-shirts! I refused to be filmed and got all demanding with the producers.

'Why are you making my life hell?'

'This isn't about you, Charlotte, it's just a new house-mate!'

'Well, I know he will have said on camera that he used to date me and it will be another reason for Mitch to be angry.'

'He hasn't even said anything about you, Charlotte . . .'

And to be fair, he hadn't. I was being a diva and over-re-acting. To this day, Kyle has never forgiven me for spoiling his entrance and making him feel unwelcome. But now he's dating Holly and it's amazing because I love them both to bits (I just have a tendency to meddle a bit too much in their relationship!).

Marnie is also a favourite of mine and I knew her before she joined, too. She's Sophie's cousin and Sophie was shocked and angry when she appeared in series seven. She said, 'Why the hell didn't you tell me you were coming in?!' Now Sophie's left it's nice having Marnie as a family representative. And there's no way Marnie's going anywhere because she's such a big character in the show – she always causes dramas. Usually over boys. She's been with Scotty T, Aaron *and* Gary. As for Aaron, he's Gary's best mate but I don't hold that against him – he's lovely. He's covered in tattoos, which makes a change from those girlie V-neck T-shirts the rest of the boys wear.

When Vicky left in series nine the house felt really empty at first. She'd been such a big character that it was a big loss – who else was going to shout at us? If you'd done something wrong she'd be the first person to let you know about it. She was like the mother figure in there. I remember one morning Holly turned to me and said, 'Do you not feel like something's really different?' and I answered, 'Yeah, I wonder what it is?' but it was because Vicky wasn't there.

My relationship with Vicky is a strange one and quite sad, now I think of it. The last time I saw her was at the after-party for the NTAs and it was a bit awkward because we hadn't really spoken for ages. I'd been used to being with her 24/7, we did everything together, but now it was clear we'd grown apart. Shortly afterwards I started reading magazine articles where she'd allegedly said I was trying to copy her career. Which was the last thing I was trying to do. So there became this whole 'Vicky and Charlotte at war!' thing and I really didn't like it.

I texted her to ask if she had really said that stuff about me and she replied, 'No, Charlotte, I would never say anything like that. My words have been twisted . . .' so I gave her the benefit of the doubt. But the one word that she'd used in the articles was 'emulated'. She was saying, 'Charlotte has emulated me.' It was a typical Vicky word and I knew she'd used it a lot before, so it made me question whether her words had been twisted after all. Anyway, no matter what she will always be part of my *Geordie* Shore family.

As for me, the DVD is still doing amazingly well. I recently heard the news that it's gone platinum – which sounds like I'm turning into a piece of jewellery. I really want to stay involved with fitness and do more DVDs because it's completely changed my life. I'm a much happier and more confident person now. I'm so much healthier and I also like seeing my body transforming. I like pushing my muscles to their limits and watching them change!

Once upon a time I never got papped by photographers, but it's amazing how much interest there is when you've lost a shitload of weight. Now there are paps everywhere and I've heard one of them admit that they've been offered massive amounts of money to get a bad picture of me! How hurtful is that? I could be the skinniest person in the world but if you caught me at a wrong angle it could look awful, and then it would be headline news: 'Charlotte's put all her weight back on.' It's like there are people waiting for me to slip up.

Thank fuck Holly and Sophie have been on diets, too! It means we can share tips and support each other. When we all went on holiday to Cape Verde together we were exercising all the time. I was showing them some of my routines from *3-Minute Belly Blitz* and they were showing me their moves on the beach. The maddest thing of all? We only had one night out drinking! We were waking up early and doing exercise every morning. One day we looked at each other and said, 'Are we the same people? What the hell is wrong with us?'

The contrast to how we used to be is massive. We were so unhealthy. Don't get me wrong, eating McDonald's at every point of the day was good while it lasted but the way we looked and our self-esteem was just awful, whereas now we have all this energy and we feel so happy in ourselves. Exercise gives you a new lease of life. I never want to be that person who's just eating takeaways all day and night, drinking constantly and having to cover up on the beach or wear baggy tops because they can't physically fit into tight ones.

Obviously it's sometimes hard balancing my fitness when I'm having fun on *Geordie Shore* but I'm managing. I just try to stick to vodka and soda or water . . . most of the time, anyway.

Anyway, when I'm forty I might just have plastic surgery

all over. I'll have a boob job because I want to see how they look when they're bigger. And if I don't like them I'll just get them taken out. I'll do a big body transformation so no one recognises me and I can do magazine articles saying, 'Look at my younger body!' I'll have to have some skin fixes because I'll have definitely gone a bit saggy down south and I'll have a nose job, too. I'll probably look like a whole different person but that's the point – I'll have two different looks in one lifetime!

Mitch and I are ready to get a house together so with a bit of luck, by the time this book's out I'll have my own pad in London with Mitch.

I've thought about what my ideal house will be like and

it won't be one of the normal ones that you draw; it will be a different shape, like maybe a rectangle. There will be lots of glass features so it has good natural light (perfect for selfies) and it will be very open-plan, with tiles and a wooden floor (no carpets because they're too hard to clean). There will be a gym and five bedrooms (so all my friends and family can stay) and a lovely big garden for garden parties. There will also be an indoor pool in the basement for even more parties.

When I'm ready to have children I'll need to make sure me mam has moved to London, too. I don't want to have to travel five hours to see her. I need her to help me have a bath as it is, so when I'm pregnant I'll need her EVERY DAY! I really must try to be a millionaire by the time I'm thirty so I can pay for me mam to be with me full time.

CHARLOTTE'S WORK BUCKET LIST

- See *Geordie Shore* win an NTA
- Go on *I'm a Celebrity Get Me Out of Here!* (I've wanted to do this since I first started watching it when I was a kid)
- Release a follow-up DVD to my *3-Minute Belly Blitz*
- See this book to go to number one (although I'm scared to even write it in case I jinx it . . .)
- Present the weather on *This Morning* (a childhood ambition to be a weathergirl!)
- Sit on a panel with Simon Cowell (I think we'd get on)
- Be interviewed by Jonathan Ross

- Have Rihanna rap one of the follow-ups to a song I sang on an Australian radio show about me weeing all the time, called 'Danger Piss'
- Perfect a party trick (something I can perform for the queen . . . which is obviously not going to be a fanny fart)
- Work with David Attenborough on anything to do with sea-life (I love narwhals!). I've always wanted to present a wildlife show and if David will have me I'll do anything – camera assistant, runner, carry his kit, even brush his hair
- Work more with Ant and Dec
- Make a difference for the charities I work with – the Anthony Nolan Trust and Barnado's and also I'd like to do more for Cancer Research
- Keep developing Nostalgia, my clothing range – this needs a bucket list of its own. I'd like to be wearing and sharing Nostalgia for all the key times of my life, e.g. marriage, maternity, children . . . (no pressure, Jamie and Adam!)

I've told Mitch that he needs to propose within the next four years, otherwise what's the point?

I've been talking to Melissa about how I want him to propose and I've decided that I'll be happy however he does it, but there just have to be a few factors taken into account:

1. No audience – I don't want anyone else around, just him and me.

2. In the two weeks building up to it, he'll have to be treating me really well; giving me extra amounts of love, buying me flowers, treating me to nice meals and buying me presents – that way I will be properly loved up with him and thinking how amazing he is when he does it. The proposal can't happen after any old normal week when we've been staying in, eating boring food and lying in bed watching *Vampire Diaries*.

3. I'd like it to be very romantic and scenic so I can get a really good picture of it for Instagram.

I have it all worked out, you see! I even have a twenty-five-year plan:

Age twenty-six: Have my own house.

Age twenty-seven: Engaged (to Mitch).

Age twenty-eight: I need to be married (to Mitch) because in a couple of years I'll start trying for a baby.

Age thirty: Pregnant. If it's a boy we'll call him Ted. We don't have a girl's name yet but Letitia is our family name so she might have to get that. I'll hopefully have my own reality TV show by then (Holly has to be in it, too) and I'll let them film all the birthing scenes like they do in *Keeping up with the Kardashians*. Saying that, I can't watch *One Born Every Minute*. It's worse than any horror film I've ever watched in my entire life.

Age thirty to thirty-two: I'll take two years off to have the parent–child bonding thing.

Age forty: Loads of plastic surgery.

Age fifty: Possibly move to Australia.

And here's how I'd like to be remembered when I die: *'She was someone who made other people laugh. She had a bit of a weak bladder but ultimately, in dark times she brought light into the world.'*

So that's it, dear reader . . . the story of my life so far. I hope you've enjoyed it and haven't got bored (I've tried to keep it to the most interesting bits so I hope you appreciate my efforts). I also hope I haven't offended you too much with my tales of wee and poo (but without those you wouldn't be getting the whole story!).

In honour of you getting to the end of this book, I've written a poem – just for you.

Here goes . . .

Well that's it, you've reached the very last bit,
So now you can finally go for a shit
Let's say our goodbyes but try not to cry
Because to say that I'm going would be a lie
So see you later, friends
Love you and take care
Meet you on the next adventure
Be there or be square ☺

THINGS I'VE LEARNT DOING THIS BOOK

1. Sometimes I'm too honest – but that's not such a bad thing.
2. I've got amazing family and great friends.
3. I should never sleep on a roof drunk.
4. I shouldn't steal a car even if it is my own.
5. I'm a very lucky girl to have so many opportunities and so much support.
6. I'm grateful that Lucie (Cave) has ghostwritten this book with me, it's been a great experience and I feel I've made a friend in the process (plus Lucie was secretly pregnant the whole time – an added blessing!).
7. A hairy fairy is OK.
8. You should always put your heart into everything and try as hard as possible – then somehow you might just make a best-selling fitness DVD.
9. A pint of Baileys and McDonald's every day will make you fat.
10. I talk about poo a lot (probably too much).
11. Things that make you cry will make you a stronger person (see Fairygate and my *Nuts* shoot before *BB*).
12. Parsnips are disgusting and never to be trusted.
13. If there's a party in the *Geordie Shore* house it will usually end up in a fight.
14. Be yourself at all times and don't tell lies.
15. When you get drunk try not to let your boyfriend near your phone because he might hack it and pretend he's proposed to you . . .

Acknowledgements

First, massive thanks to Lucie Cave for being an amazing ghostwriter, and Sarah Emsley, Holly Harris and all at Headline for letting this book be so Me (Me Me).

Also thanks to Kate O'Shea for being a great agent, as well as Martin O'Shea, Joe Foster, Jade Reuben, Jackie Christian and all the team at Bold Management, and Francis Ridley and Dana Malmstrom at Money Management. Thank you Luke Mills for being a good friend, and working so closely with my team!

To Steve Regan, Craig Orr, Kerri Taylor, Roberta Duman and all at MTV, thanks for believing in me and for the amazing opportunity of *Geordie Shore*! Lauren Benson – thanks for finding me. Also thanks to Jake Attwell, Kate Bates and all at Lime Pictures.

Everyone at Channel 5 and *Celebrity Big Brother*: thanks for the experience, the opportunities and the new friends.

Emily Hudd, Iain Wimbush, Lucy Rothery and all at Rumpus; Sarah Thornton, Mark Proctor, Kate Kielty and all the team at TLC: thank you for letting Charlotte Columbus roam the world meeting such different communities!

Shane Tyler, Ben Grand and all at Stage Addiction, thanks for all things Australian!

Last but not least huge thanks to all my crazy, wonderful fans for being able to handle my utter weirdness and for supporting me through thick and thin – it honestly means the world to me!

Picture Credits